The Superintendent's Guide to Controlling Putting Green Speed

Thomas A. Nikolai, Ph.D.

WILEY

John Wiley & Sons, Inc.

Copyright © 2005 by John Wiley & Sons, Inc. All rights reserved

Published by John Wiley & Sons, Inc., Hoboken, New Jersey
Published simultaneously in Canada

For general information on our other products and services or for technical support, please contact our Customer Care Department within the United States at (800) 762-2974, outside the United States at (317) 572-3993 or fax (317) 572-4002.

Wiley also publishes its books in a variety of electronic formats. Some content that appears in print may not be available in electronic books. For more information about Wiley products, visit our web site at www.wiley.com.

Library of Congress Cataloging-in-Publication Data:
Nikolai, Thomas, 1959-
  The superintendent's guide to controlling putting green speed / Thomas Nikolai.
    p. cm.
  Includes bibliographical references.
  ISBN 0-471-47272-7
  1. Golf courses—Maintenance. 2. Turf management. I. Title.
  GV975.5.N54 2004
  796.352′06′8—dc22
2004011074

Printed in the United States of America
10 9 8 7 6 5 4 3 2

To all golf course superintendents who have heard that their greens were too fast and too slow on the same day. I hope this book is helpful.

Contents

4

The Weather: The Known Unknown in the Quest for the Ideal Green Speed

5

Putting Green Root Zones

6

Turfgrass Species and Green Speed

7

Mowing Height

8

Fertilization and Green Speed

9

Lightweight Rolling: A Most Vexing Practice for Many Superintendents

10

An Integrated Approach to Green Speed Management and Tournament Preparation

11

Filling in the Missing Pieces

Preface

This book is designed to serve as a guide for the golf course superintendent on most every topic pertaining to green speed. It was the intention
of Eddie Stimpson and Al Radko that the release of the Stimpmeter would
help golf to become a more enjoyable game. Since its release in 1978
there have been numerous studies that have utilized the Stimpmeter to
make green speed measurements, but until now there has not been
enough data generated to warrant a book on the subject. It is my hope
that this text stimulates further dialogue between superintendents,
golfers, and turfgrass researchers to further our understanding of the factors affecting green speed.

I am extremely fortunate to have been the research technician of Paul
E. Rieke at Michigan State University. For ten years Paul was my mentor; he
also valued my opinions and gave me freedom to create studies and gather
green speed data on research plots with his Stimpmeter. Thank you, Paul.

I would like to acknowledge Peter Cookingham and the great job he
and his staff have done with indexing and creating the turfgrass database
known as the Turfgrass Information File (TGIF). I would also like to thank
the United States Golf Association, the O.J. Noer Foundation, and J.B.
Beard for their financial support and literary contributions to the TGIF.
The TGIF was an enormous asset in the writing of this book.

In addition, there are many persons who have contributed to this book,
and I quote them liberally so that the reader will be assured that the information is not solely my opinion. When I felt it was necessary, I attempted to clarify what might appear to be conflicting results from similar
research studies, and I certainly hope I did not take anyone's work out
of context. I cite the data and comments of others so that the more in-
quisitive reader can look further into a specific topic (the TGIF may be
very helpful).

I would like to acknowledge the enormous support that the Michigan Turfgrass Foundation has given me over the years. Moreover, I would like to thank the Michigan State University Turfgrass faculty and staff in the writing of this text, most notably Joe Vargas Jr., John "Trey" Rogers III, and Ron Calhoun for their continued encouragement.

Thanks also to the numerous golf course assistants and superintendents for their conversations over the phone, in the hallways at the venues, and, when I was fortunate enough, on the courses. A special thanks to Mike Morris, CGCS, Crystal Downs Country Club. I would also like to thank my wife, Michele, for her understanding when I canceled the trip to Mackinac Island in the fall and the ski trip over winter break to work on this book. Finally, I would like to thank my children, Joshua, Anya, and Delaney, for being easy on Mom when I was gone all those nights and weekends.

Introduction

Speed does *not* kill grass! Haste, ignorance, stubbornness, complacency, and rash, uninformed decisions may kill grass, but speed does not. You now have two clear choices: (1) You can put this book down and go on reading articles about the perils of green speed that are written with the worthy intention of giving the superintendent ammunition in green committee meetings, or (2) you can read on and become the green speed authority at your golf course.

For more than 100 years, the speed of a putting surface has been an issue in the game of golf. Most often a golfer has initiated the debate about green speed, putting the golf course superintendent in a defensive position. The intent of this book is to define clearly what is known, as well as the misconceptions, about green speed by examining data obtained from research facilities and golf courses throughout the world. The comments of various golf course superintendents regarding green speed and management practices are interspersed throughout the chapters. It will become clear to the reader that I subscribe to the clichés "We can't know where we are going if we don't know where we have been" and "Those who do not know history are cursed to repeat it."

Articles in trade magazines about green speed seem to suggest that a superintendent can either manage his or her greens for speed or manage them for healthy turf. The premise seems to be that both aims cannot be accomplished. I strongly disagree. It is my belief that if a superintendent is not managing for an "ideal green speed," then he or she may be missing out on the best way to manage the greens.

This book is designed to help the superintendent find his or her ideal green speed and to determine how best to stay within its bounds.

It has been more than 25 years since the release of the Stimpmeter, and it is time that this equipment is used for its intended purpose. It is time to recognize that managing for green speed is an obtainable goal and that staying within an ideal green speed is a reasonable objective.

Problems Associated with Green Speed

Nature abhors straight lines, uniformity, and regularity.
Golf was originally played on land unaltered by the hand
of man. To regain the original charm of the game a golf
course should abound in curves, variations, and
simple irregularities.
ANONYMOUS, 1929

What Is Green Speed?

According to a Golf Course Superintendents Association of America (GC-SAA) survey, golfers consider green speed the number one factor to know about a golf course (*USA Today*, 2002). This fact alone indicates that golf course superintendents need a thorough knowledge of the factors that impact green speed. Unfortunately, deciphering the facts and fiction of green speed is no easy task.

Webster's standard reference dictionary does not define the term *green speed*, but the words *green* and *speed* have been unseparable in turfgrass writing for more than a century (ever since the rubber-cored golf ball replaced the gutta ball at the dawn of the twentieth century). "Green speed" typically indicates either how fast, or how far, a golf ball travels after it has been struck with a putter. Clearly, when the golfer is involved, the determination is highly subjective.

When a golfer feels that he or she has struck the golf ball with the proper impact and the golf ball ends up short of the hole, then the speed

1

FIGURE 1-1. *Undoubtedly there are some golfers who would think that this green is too slow, since the putt stopped short of the cup.*

of the green is considered slow (Figure 1-1). But, had the perfectly struck golf ball quickly rimmed the cup and not fallen in or rolled way past the hole, missing the intended break, the green would be considered fast. However, when the perfectly struck ball does indeed fall into the cup or comes to rest pin-high (indicating that the putt may have been slightly misread), the green speed is considered perfect. So, to the golfer, "green speed" is synonymous with how fast and/or how far the ball travels.

In 1937, Eddie Stimpson wrote, "It occurred to us that there was no way of measuring how fast putting greens are," which was the catalyst for the invention of the Stimpmeter (Stimpson, 1937). Today the Stimpmeter is the universally accepted method of quantifying green speed. In fact, the Stimpmeter and green speed have become inseparable, as *green speed* has been defined as "a term used to describe the distance a ball travels on a golf putting green when released from an inclined plane called a Stimpmeter" (Hartwiger et al., 2001).

I offer the following definitions of green speed:

1. The perceived swiftness with which (or distance to which) a golf ball travels across the putting surface after it has been struck with a putter by a golfer

2

2. The average distance of six golf balls (three rolled in one direction and three rolled in the opposite direction) released from a Stimpmeter (or possibly any other agreed-upon inclined plane) on a golf course putting green

3. The following speeds of a ball, as measured with a Stimpmeter (USGA, 1996):

> Fast, more than 8.5 feet; medium, between 7.5 and 8.5 feet; slow, less than 7.5 feet—for regular membership play

> Fast, more than 9.5 feet; medium, between 8.5 and 9.5 feet; slow, less than 8.5 feet—for tournament play

The three definitions are accurate enough for our communication purposes. However, they create a conundrum, because although all the definitions may indeed be true, they can also conflict. Certainly, definition 1 is not always in agreement with definition 3, and definition 2 can be used to refute parties subscribing to definitions 1 and/or 3. This is part of the predicament for the golf course superintendent.

The Best Laid Plans

The Stimpmeter in its present form was first released in 1978. One of the goals of having a device to quantifiably measure green speed was to set limits on the speed of severely contoured greens so that the golfer would have fair pin placements. Even though the United States Golf Association (USGA) warned that green speeds were not to be used for comparing courses, golfers demanded speeds equivalent to, or in excess of, those of neighboring clubs and in some cases wanted speeds they learned about while watching the PGA Tour on the weekend.

Some golf course superintendents have pushed the limits of turfgrass agronomy by decreasing the height of cut, fertilization, and irrigation without any valid research to guide them. Some, through trial and error, found success and contributed to how greens are managed today; others lost their jobs because agronomic errors caused them to lose grass or they were unable to produce the demanded speed. To this day, superintendents continue to experiment with management practices and/or products that supposedly increase green speed. Often these efforts are nothing more than a waste of both time and money.

In addition, the USGA, which released and refined the Stimpmeter, preaches about the perils of fast greens. Many superintendents would be

3

happy to heed these cautions, but in many cases, such warnings fall on deaf ears in green committee meetings. Other superintendents have stated that they want the USGA to "get up to speed." Articles advising against green speeds faster than 10 feet are of little value to the superintendent who is paid to meet the demands of creating faster green speeds.

One of the original goals of the creation and release of the Stimpmeter was to allow fair pin placements on sloped areas; however, there is a current trend to "smooth out" the traditionally preferred contoured putting surfaces—all in the name of increasing green speed. Confusion, rather than communication, reigns. The question is, Why?

Researcher-Superintendent Communication Problems

In many respects, the superintendent has gotten little help besides the warning, "speed kills," meaning that it kills turf. Even when research has produced data that validates a safe method to increase green speed, a disclaimer is invariably attached, warning of the perils of fast greens. I must confess that I, too, have done this. I believe that there are two reasons for such caveats: (1) Space is limited for trade journal articles, and the writer often cannot thoroughly cover the intricacies of why some methods may or may not work on particular golf courses, and (2) no one wants to be blamed for dead turf. Thus, although the disclaimer "speed kills" is used with the best of intentions, it leaves a mixed message and, invariably, the superintendent holding the bag.

Moreover, a researcher knows that a proposal to study the intricacies of putting green speed must compete with other, perhaps more popular, endeavors in securing a research grant. For this reason, there is still a great deal of research that must be done regarding green speed.

Almost everyone has an opinion on green speed, and there are many people who are perpetuating the myths. Yet there are few who have treated green speed as a researchable issue. No one is really to blame, because all are well intentioned, but this is part of the reason that so many misconceptions regarding green speed persist.

To add to the confusion, when most turfgrass researchers present or write about data regarding green speed, they often use the term "ball roll distance" (I'm guilty here) because it is more scientifically accurate. "How can we call it green speed," they question, "when the Stimpmeter measures *distance*?" This is true, but the same individuals often add the disclaimer "speed kills" in their papers, and the truth is that speed does not kill turf.

The vast majority of articles on the subject inform the superintendent about the perils of ever-increasing green speeds instead of giving pertinent information on *how* to manage their greens for speed. Furthermore, many articles make generalized statements that are flat-out incorrect and/or unsubstantiated.

Finally, consider the misinformation that is often spread during weekend golf on television. This erroneous information, given by well-intentioned, nonreliable sources, is repeated at green committee meetings, and the superintendent has few trusted sources to clarify the misinformation.

Given this entire scenario, it is little wonder that many superintendents pretend that they do not have a Stimpmeter and that others falsely inflate their green speeds to appease their clubs' membership.

Whose Golf Course Is It Anyway?

Joe Vargas of Michigan State University teaches his turfgrass students that, "if the members want you to dig a 4 by 4 by 4-foot hole in the middle of number one fairway, your job is to do it." The point is that, after all, it is the members' golf course, not the superintendent's. The golf course superintendent is an employee of the golf course and has the responsibility of managing the grounds in a condition specified by the members.

When it comes to green speed, it can be near impossible for the superintendent to give the golfers the specified conditions. On the very same day that some golfers think the greens are too fast, other golfers think they are too slow. This variance alone clearly indicates a need for the superintendent to be in charge of the issue.

Certainly, there are numerous golf course superintendents who have been confounded by the desires of the golf course membership. Many superintendents originally went into the occupation because they wanted to work outdoors and to deal with meetings as little as possible. Sitting in and communicating during committee meetings were not among their objectives. According to a survey of USGA agronomists, the superintendent's inability to communicate was the "major sin committed by those involved in golf course maintenance" (Blais, 1991). So, although it may be more pleasant to deal with their favorite golfers and avoid the others, superintendents should be able to communicate effectively with all golfers.

In order to achieve what is best for the turf, it is vitally important that the superintendent be well versed on the subject. Because the members want what is best for their club too, such knowledge should be communicated to them.

The following are the three main points covered so far:

1. Green speed is the number one factor a golfer wants to know in regard to the condition of a golf course.
2. There are numerous misconceptions regarding green speed.
3. A golf course superintendent's inability to effectively communicate with his or her clientele (i.e., green committee, board, owner(s), golfers) has been pinpointed as the biggest problem between the superintendent and the clientele.

An examination of these three points leads to the conclusion that "the issue of green speed provides an opportunity for superintendents to shine as professionals, and to offer answers to this age-old debate" (Morris, verbal communication, 2002). Ultimately, the superintendent who is well versed on issues of green speed, citing research and articulating the facts through examples and common sense, will earn the respect of his or her clientele. But the superintendent who goes into a green committee meeting and says, "Speed kills" is not communicating very effectively.

The History of Measuring Green Speed

We used to roll them with iron rollers, blasting down the
soil so that no grass could grow through it, no ball would
stop on it, and no putting was possible on it. All putting
was reduced to trickling, and the golfer who followed the
gallant old maxim of "going for the back of the hole"
would run nearly off the green unless he caught the back
of the hole very fair and square indeed.
HUTCHINSON, 1906

The Development of the Stimpmeter

In 1937, Eddie Stimpson first wrote about the Stimpmeter in an article entitled "Introducing the Stimp." The Stimpmeter was not the first device invented that attempted to measure green speed, but it has enjoyed the greatest longevity because its inventor recognized that a universally accepted device to quantitatively measure green speed must be simple to use. In his 1937 article, Stimpson noted that any device that measured green speed "should be easily carried, not take long to make measurements, must be usable on a slope, and it must require neither time nor skill to learn how to use." Within reason, the Stimpmeter fulfills these requirements.

The original Stimpmeter was a grooved wooden stick approximately 30 inches in length. Near one end, a notch was carved into the wooden U-shaped groove to hold a golf ball. When the wooden stick was lifted slowly, the ball would leave the notch at the same angle every time, thus rolling down the inclined stick at the same speed every time it was used. Given that the ball left the Stimpmeter at the same speed every time, the farther the ball rolled across the surface of the green, the faster the green speed, and vice versa. Though Stimpson wrote about his invention in 1937, it was not used regularly for another 40 years.

In the 1970s, Al Radko, national director of the U.S. Golf Association (USGA) Green Section, asked Frank Thomas, technical director at the USGA, to make a device that could accurately measure green speed. Thomas "designed four different instruments, each with an intricate ball release mechanism. These were all relatively complex designs with built-in potential for operator error" (Thomas, 1983).

Not satisfied with these designs, Mr. Thomas realized that the concept of the Stimpmeter was good, but he believed that it also had potential for operator error. Therefore, Thomas modified the Stimpmeter. The changes included a more precisely cut ball release notch, increasing the length of the Stimpmeter from 30 to 36 inches, the use of aluminum instead of wood in manufacturing to reduce cost, and replacement of the U-shaped groove with a V-shaped groove, thus reducing the friction on the ball as it traveled down the Stimpmeter. These modifications increased the distance the golf ball traveled once it was released from the notch. It is noteworthy that on the original wooden Stimpmeter, a 30-inch scale was marked "to measure the distance that the ball usually rolls, 1 to 4 feet" (Stimpson, 1937).

In the mid-1970s, the USGA tested the Stimpmeter on more than 1500 golf courses in 36 states (Radko, 1978). At that time, the average green speed was 6 feet, 6 inches. A result of these numerous green speed measurements was the development of speed charts (see Table 2-1) for regular and tournament play. The original speed charts, published in 1977, have changed very little over the years, even though it was originally stated that they "may require revision at some future date as the data used to develop [them] is limited and insufficient to be considered reliable" (Radko, 1977).

The release of speed charts, and of the Stimpmeter itself, was not haphazard; indeed, the USGA "agonized about making the Stimpmeter available to all clubs, because [it] felt it might cause problems through misuse" (Radko, 1985). Soon after its release, numerous articles appeared that validated the USGA's concerns about misuse of the Stimpmeter and the speed charts. Comments such as "I cannot help but feel that Stimpmeters are anti-grass" (Albaugh, 1983) and "We have found that we spend approxi-

TABLE 2-1

Speed Charts Developed by the USGA (based on data from tests performed by USGA Green Section agronomists over two years)

Speeds for Regular Membership Play	
8'6"	Fast
7'6"	Medium-fast
6'6"	Medium
5'6"	Medium-slow
4'6"	Slow
Speeds for Tournament Play	
10'6"	Fast
9'6"	Medium-fast
8"6"	Medium
7'6"	Medium-slow
6'6"	Slow

mately four times the number of hours (and expense) on putting green mower maintenance than we did only a few years ago" (Mitchell, 1983) attest to the immediate impact the Stimpmeter had on the golf course.

Perhaps no one has spoken more clearly about the impact of the Stimpmeter on golf than Al Radko himself, the man who requested the USGA to develop an instrument to measure green speed. In 1977, Radko was writing about potential benefits of the USGA's Speedstick (a name given to the Stimpmeter for a short time). By the early 1980s, he was writing articles about the abuse of the Stimpmeter: "Now it appears that many clubs are attempting tournament speeds for the entire playing season. This, in my opinion, places putting green management in a totally new category, with risks far greater than greens were ever subjected to before." Furthermore, Radko noted that there were agronomic problems resulting from this need for speed, including increased "moss, algae, silver crabgrass, and undesirable encroachment; thin, stringy turf; decumbent rather than upright growth; turf lacking turgidity, thatch, and density; many more ball marks with displaced turf; more scalping over terraces, mounds, and crests of slopes; decidedly a weak, off-color appearance, not a healthy look; weaker turf in summer; weaker turf in winter, which could add to winter injury problems and also mean slower spring recovery that could affect length of playing

time" (Radko, 1985). It appears that he felt a little like Dr. Franken-
stein felt about his creation.

Yet, Eddie Stimpson, Al Radko, and Frank Thomas should be proud of
their roles in creating a device to measure green speed on the putting
surface. They were always aware of the fact that if their tool was in the
wrong hands (the golfers), there was potential for abuse. It was precisely
for that reason that Stimpmeters could only be mailed to golf courses in
care of the superintendent (Radko, 1978).

However, soon after its release, the Stimpmeter was in the hands of
club members. In 1983, the superintendent at Westmoreland Country
Club, Wilmette, Illinois, wrote the following about a golfer:

> In his spare time he visited a club or two a day, some in the mornings, others
> at night. He made some readings after a heavy rain, others under the driest of
> conditions. He did not know if the green had been mowed that day or double
> cut. He did not know the turfgrass variety or the height of cut. He did not
> know anything except how to roll a ball down an aluminum bar. When he had
> finished his readings, he compiled his so-called expert data and proceeded to
> hassle the golf course superintendent at his home course (Albaugh, 1983).

It appears that the speed charts were a major contributor to the dis-
like of the Stimpmeter by many superintendents, as their "fears had to
do with competition of speed of greens—between clubs with nothing
else in common" (Mitchell, 1983). Certainly, categorizing greens as fast
to slow, as the speed charts do, would result in very few golfers requesting
slow greens.

Many people prefer fast cars, and they also admire the fine lines and
aerodynamic curves of an automobile. I have often wondered, what if the
original speed charts had been called "Contour Distance Charts" and were
published to reflect the topography of greens (Table 2-2)? The information in the charts would have been generally the same but would have
been presented in a manner that takes away from the premise that fast
is preferred, because fast greens would have also been associated with
flat greens.

New Technology

Although the speed charts may be partially to blame for accelerating green
speed, it was inevitable that green speeds would increase when they did,
with or without the Stimpmeter. It just so happens that the release of the

TABLE 2-2
Hypothetical Contour Distance Charts

Speeds for Regular Membership Play	
8'6"	Flat
7'6"	Single slope
6'6"	Multiple slopes
5'6"	Moderately contoured
4'6"	Severely contoured
Speeds for Tournament Play	
10'6"	Flat
9'6"	Single slope
8"6"	Multiple slopes
7'6"	Moderately contoured
6'6"	Severely contoured

Stimpmeter coincided with new technology that allowed bedknives to be manufactured thinner. For most of the 1970s, the tightest a stand of grass could be mowed was 3/16 of an inch, because the thickness of the bedknives would not allow turf to be cut lower. Incidentally, this is the same height of cut at which a superintendent could have been mowing greens in 1930.

In 1977, Al Radko wrote, "Superior greens reduce the element of luck to a minimum and putting becomes a true test of skill." Although the Stimpmeter may have gotten off to a rocky start, over the years it has changed management practices and provided the golfer with many benefits.

In 1983, Robert Mitchell, CGCS, noted that the ability to measure green speed changed his management practices, including

> frequent light vertical mowing every two weeks instead of heavy monthly vertical mowings. We also mow our greens seven days a week instead of six or less. Frequent light topdressings are accomplished every three or four weeks instead of three or four times annually. Light, frequent fertilizer applications are made and provide slow, steady growth and recovery from player damage. We water as infrequently as the grass will allow, but enough to retain color and resiliency to hold a well executed shot. We avoid frequent saturations. It is essential to mechanically check and service green mowers daily as opposed to a haphazard schedule. And there are other points. But please note that these same procedures will also produce the quality of turf so necessary to answer the demands of today's golfer, and at the same time, permit us close mowing.

Today, many superintendents adhere to similar management practices that Mitchell attributed to the invention of the Stimpmeter. However, there are still many concerns regarding the ability to measure green speed, as well as golfer demands to have the fastest greens. Although it is true that a club's membership, with the guidance of the green committee and, in some cases, sole ownership, may rightfully have final say on matters concerning green speed, it is our job, mine as a researcher and yours as a golf course superintendent, to give them the best information to make a good decision. Currently, some old traditional golf courses are "smoothing out" their greens to increase their Stimpmeter measurements. Others are killing off the grass on their greens and converting to newer species to increase green speeds. For the preservation of golf's past, and common sense in the present, it is time for the superintendent to take control of green speed.

3

Using the Stimpmeter for Its Intended Purpose: Creating the Ideal Green Speed

With a unit of measurement and a means of measuring the speed of greens well within the cost of every club there is no reason why the better courses cannot work toward a standard ideal green speed for their greens.
EDDIE STIMPSON, 1937

Twenty-Five-Year Anniversary

High hopes for improved playing conditions accompanied the release of the Stimpmeter, yet several years later numerous articles appeared that condemned the Stimpmeter and the U.S. Golf Association (USGA) itself began cautioning about the perils of ever-increasing green speeds.

It has been more than 25 years since the release of the Stimpmeter, and this seems an appropriate time to look back at the intended purpose of the tool and evaluate its promise for the golf course superintendent.

Uniformity

Uniformity was a major objective in the creation of the Stimpmeter, and in terms of green speed uniformity can be divided into two areas: (1) uniform speeds from green to green on a particular golf course and (2)

13

uniform speeds on different areas of the same green. Let us consider each area separately.

Uniformity 1

In 1937, Eddie Stimpson wrote: "The most enjoyable courses to play are those with greens which have a minimum variation in speed." Uniform speeds from green to green on a particular course means having the same green speed on all 18 holes for play. The question then is, "What is uniformity from green to green?"

Addressing this question, golfer perception surveys (Figure 3-1) indicate two interesting points: (1) golfers cannot detect differences in green speed of 6 inches or less on adjacent putting greens, and (2) while the majority of golfers can detect differences in green speed up to a foot, as the green speed increases, their ability to detect 1-foot differences in speed diminishes (Karcher et al, 2001).

Therefore, playing it safe would dictate that uniform speeds are achieved when all 18 greens result in Stimpmeter measurements within 6 inches of one another. Maintaining green speeds within 6 inches of one

FIGURE 3-1. *Kevin Frank and Brandon Horvath wait behind the green to take a survey of the golfers in regard to green speed. When the golfers have finished putting, they will be asked, "Which green do you think was faster, this one or the one on the previous hole?" Surveys of golfers' perceptions of green speed taken on research plots and adjacent golf course greens indicate that golfers cannot detect differences in green speed of 6 inches or less, but have little trouble in detecting a 1-foot difference in green speed.*

another is a normal practice utilized for tournament play. (I have been informed that PGA Tour Pros can tell differences in green speed as little as 4 inches, and while I do not discount this claim, I have not been privy to the data that verifies it.) In normal day-to-day golf course operations, it is safe to assume that as green speeds become greater than 9.5 feet, uniformity may be considered to be achieved when all the greens are within 1 foot of one another.

Uniformity 2

Clearly, gravity dictates that a ball will roll faster (or farther) down a slope than it would if rolled on a flat surface or up the same slope. Thus, *uniformity* on all areas of the same green may seem like a misnomer. However, uniformity in this context refers to ensuring fair playing conditions in regard to pin placement.

In preparing for the release of the Stimpmeter, USGA Green Section director Al Radko in 1977 wrote, "A hole should be placed in such a position that no matter where the golfer is putting from, assuming continuous putting surface between himself and the hole, it should be possible to stop the ball within approximately two feet of the hole." He further noted, "A hole location which presented a fair challenge when the green speed was approximately six and one half feet may quite possibly be a very bad position when the green speed is eight or nine feet, assuming, as an example, this position to be on or at the bottom of [a] sloping portion of the green" (see Figure 3-2).

Therefore, an expressed purpose of the Stimpmeter was to aid in pin placements to improve playing conditions on contoured greens. This mandate is still reflected in the Stimpmeter instruction booklet: "A green so fast (or a hole cut in such a position) that a ball cannot be stopped near the hole from any point on the green, for example, is an unfair challenge" (USGA, 1996).

To further consider Uniformity 2, it is helpful to consult the Stimpmeter instruction booklet and its two directives.

The Two Directives

The Stimpmeter instruction booklet includes what I consider to be two implied directives for using the Stimpmeter. These two directives do not

FIGURE 3-2. *Slopes should be taken into consideration prior to setting the cup to make sure the location is fair. (Image compliments of Dr. Kevin Frank, Michigan State University)*

appear next to each other in the booklet, but it is my contention that, taken together, they constitute an important guide to the intended use of the Stimpmeter.

1. The Stimpmeter is not intended for course comparisons.
2. It is *not* the intention of the USGA to attempt to standardize green speeds, which should remain up to course officials, with the input of the superintendent, of each individual facility.

You may have already seen these two directives. If so, and if, in addition, you did something to comply with them, you are in a very small minority who have taken control of green speed at their golf courses, unless of course, the scenario went something like this:

The setting: A green committee meeting

The current agenda topic: Green speed

GREEN COMMITTEE CHAIR: I was playing at my buddy's golf course last week, and he told me his greens' Stimp was an 11.

COMMITTEE MEMBER 1: That doesn't seem very fast compared to the tournament on TV last weekend when the announcer said the greens were "Stimping at 13."

GOLF COURSE SUPERINTENDENT: That may be all well and fine, but the Stimpmeter is not intended for course comparisons.

ALL COMMITTEE MEMBERS (*LAUGHING*): That's silly . . . doesn't make sense . . .

SUPERINTENDENT: No, really, Stimpmeter readings are not comparable from one golf course to the next.

CHAIR: Why? I mean, isn't 25 miles per hour always 25 miles per hour?

SUPERINTENDENT: Why, yes, I suppose it is.

MEMBER 1: Then an 11 must always be an 11 as measured with a Stimpmeter, right?

SUPERINTENDENT: Well, yes, I guess so.

COMMITTEE MEMBER 2: There you have it; then there must be nothing wrong with course comparisons.

CHAIR: In that case, we should have green speeds of 11 every day.

SUPERINTENDENT: But the Stimpmeter instruction booklet, which was written by the USGA, says that the green speed at this course should be determined by course officials with the aid of the superintendent.

CHAIR: Yes, indeed. Very well, then, all in favor of having green speeds in excess of 11 every day signify by saying, "Aye."

ALL COMMITTEE MEMBERS: Aye.

CHAIR: All opposed, say, "Nay."

SUPERINTENDENT: Nay.

CHAIR: "The ayes have it, the motion passes; our green speed should be at least an 11 every day.

SUPERINTENDENT: But speed kills.

MEMBER 2: It didn't kill the greens at Flat-top Ridge.

SUPERINTENDENT: But their greens are flat, our greens have a lot of contours.

MEMBER 1: Then take out the slopes.

SUPERINTENDENT: But this is a Donald Ross course.

MEMBER 2: No, it isn't, it's our course.

What may be needed here are a couple of analogies that can help the superintendent in the preceding scene explain the two directives.

Directive 1: The Stimpmeter is not intended for course comparisons

Clearly, golfers, TV golf analysts, turfgrass agronomists, and even golf course superintendents fail to follow Directive 1 more often than not. Granted, it is hard to resist the temptation to compare golf courses, and it is exceedingly difficult to comprehend why a green speed of 10 feet at one golf course should not be compared with a speed of 10 feet at another golf course. To understand why green speeds should not be compared from course to course, consider the following analogy.

A lone driver on a western desert road, driving toward a distant majestic mountain range, delights at the wide-open spaces and the exhilarating feeling of driving 80 miles an hour. As the driver approaches the base of the mountains, the road begins to have long, sloping curves as the flat surface of the desert is left behind. As the driver gets closer still to the mountains, there are hills and valleys and even more long, sloping curves.

Finally, the driver enters a mountain pass, where treacherous hairpin turns mean that one miscue at the wheel could result in a fatal error. At this point, the thought of traveling at 80 miles an hour is long gone, but the exhilaration of the drive has not diminished. In fact, some would say, the true exhilaration and test of driving skills are found in the mountain pass.

It is true that 80 miles an hour is 80 miles an hour in any terrain, but that does not mean that driving a car at 80 miles an hour is always warranted. In fact, 35 miles an hour on the hairpin curves of the mountain pass may actually be more exhilarating and may indeed even seem faster than the 80 miles an hour experienced on the flat desert road (Figure 3-3).

So it may also be true that 10 feet on a Stimpmeter is always 10 feet. And, likewise, given the topography of the green, a 10-foot speed may seem slow, or fast, or downright dangerous. Therefore, just as different contours, surfaces, and maintenance practices dictate the driving speed on our roadways' different contours, the surfaces and maintenance practices of different golf courses should dictate their green speeds. It is precisely for this reason that Directive 1 states that the Stimpmeter is not intended for course comparisons.

FIGURE 3-3 (*a–d*). *Just as different slopes, contours, and maintenance practices dictate the rates of speed for automobile traffic, so too do slopes, contours, and maintenance practices dictate green speed.*

Directive 2: It is not the intention of the USGA to attempt to standardize green speeds, which should remain up to course officials, with the input of the superintendent, of each individual facility

Directive 2 is probably not misused as much as it is totally ignored, and it implies that each golf course should decide what its ideal green speed should be. This directive is part of the vision that Eddie Stimpson had when he created the Stimpmeter, as in 1937 he wrote that with "a means of measuring the speed of greens well within the cost of every club there is no reason why the better courses cannot work toward a standard ideal green speed for their greens."

19

The greatest problem with Directive 2 is that it did not come with a set of concrete instructions. For instance, how do course officials decide the "ideal green speed" for their golf course? Fortunately, there is a tested method that has led to positive results. I call it the "Morris Method." Although there may be various other approaches, I offer the Morris Method as a way to determine your golf course greens' ideal speed.

The Morris Method

During the late summer of 2000, Mike Morris, CGCS, of Crystal Downs Country Club in Frankfort, Michigan, phoned and asked me, "Is it possible to have the same green speed on the golf course for the entire playing season?" Crystal Downs is a very exclusive country club that is normally ranked in the Top 25 golf courses in America. Therefore, I figured that if anyone could pull off this feat, Mike at Crystal Downs could. However, my reply was, "The easy answer is no—but the better one is, let's find out."

A study was set up at Crystal Downs Country Club in the spring of 2001. It was determined that we would need to gather green speed measurements twice daily on two different greens on the golf course. We also needed two separate weather stations near each green to gather data regarding the impact of the weather on green speed. In addition, because the goal was to have a consistent green speed from day to day, then the green speed would have to be the "ideal green speed." Thus, the question arose, How does one establish an ideal green speed? There were no explicit directions on how to determine an ideal green speed for a particular golf course.

It was decided that we needed to survey some golfers after they had completed their rounds of golf. Mike took this idea to his green committee; at first there was some resistance, but it soon became clear that this was the only way to establish the course's ideal green speed.

The survey was very simple, which is important for success. After completing a round of golf, the golfer was given a card. The golfer's task was to fill in the date and then simply circle one of five replies, indicating whether he or she thought that the greens were Too Slow, Slow/OK, OK, Fast/OK, or Too Fast. Figure 3-4 shows a simple survey form a golfer can fill out after finishing his or her round of golf to help determine the ideal green speed at the golf course.

Of course, the golfers had no idea what the Stimpmeter reading was for the day, but Mike, the superintendent, did. After receiving the daily surveys from the golfers, he wrote the average green speed of the day on the cards, and after several months the data was compiled and presented to the green committee in graph form.

The results for Crystal Downs Country Club were that 81% of the golfers surveyed rated the green speed as OK or Fast/OK when the speeds as measured were in the range of 9 feet 6 inches to 10 feet 6 inches. Thus, the ideal green speed for Crystal Downs Country Club was determined to be within this range. This speed is *not* comparable to that of any other course; it is *their* speed, as determined by the golfers and the course officials, with the valuable input of the golf course superintendent.

An Ideal Green Speed: What's in It for You?

Maybe the Morris Method seems like too much work. Maybe there are several scratch golfers on your green committee who would never go for something like a golfer/green speed survey. Maybe the club pro wouldn't like it. But consider: What's in it for you and your golf course?

Bringing the idea of establishing an ideal green speed to the green committee demonstrates that the superintendent wants to do what is best for the golf course. It clearly shows the membership that the superintendent desires to create the best possible playing conditions for the majority of golfers on a daily basis.

Date_____ The green speed during my round was . . . . Please circle one:				
Too Slow	Slow/OK	OK	Fast/OK	Too Fast

FIGURE 3-4. *Green speed survey.*

Originally, a green committee may vote "No" to the creation of an ideal green speed. After all, individuals may fear that an ideal green speed so established may be a green speed they do not want. Perhaps they will think it is a good idea as long as they are the only ones who are surveyed. Of course, common sense dictates for a long-term ideal green speed to result, a representative sample of club members must be included in the survey.

Surveys can be set up identically to those used in the Morris Method, or perhaps your method of questioning will be slightly different. Over the time period in which Mike surveyed his golfers, his green speeds ranged from 8 to 12 feet and he set up green speed categories on the ½ foot (i.e., every 6 inches). His final green speed categories were 8, 8½, 9, 9½, 10, 10½, 11, 11½, and 12 feet. Certainly, on the majority of days his Stimpmeter reading was not precisely one of those speeds. He simply rounded the number up or down to fit a given category. For example, if the Stimpmeter measurement was 10 feet 4 inches, it was considered to be 10 feet 6 inches, and if the Stimp reading was 9 feet 2 inches, it was placed in the 9 feet category for golfer responses.

Once an ideal green speed is agreed upon, it will bring to an end a lot of second-guessing. It will be clear to everyone that the golf course superintendent is attempting to manage the golf course to a specified standard. Everyone will know that the superintendent knows, on a daily basis, what the green speed is, and whether it is within, below, or above the ideal green speed as determined by the golfers.

Certainly, the golf superintendent cannot stay within the ideal green speed on a daily basis. Mike Morris stayed within the Crystal Downs ideal green speed 65 percent of the time in 2001 and 50 percent of the time in 2002. In the late spring and early summer of 2003, most likely because of poor growing conditions (cold nights and cool daytime temperatures), the green speed was normally above the ideal green speed. The result was that the green committee asked Mike to slow down the green speed. Mike decided to raise the mowing height a little, add a little more nitrogen, and ease off rolling the greens a bit until the conditions for grass growth improved.

It is noteworthy that as of late summer 2003, the Crystal Downs Green Committee was considering lowering the ideal green speed by 6 inches for the next year. That is, instead of having an ideal green speed of 9½ to 10½ feet in 2004, it is considering lowering it to 9 to 10 feet. The committee members do not see a need for another survey since they now have a better understanding of green speed on their greens.

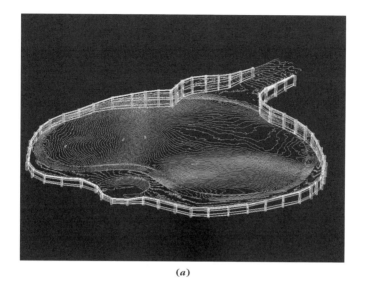

(a)

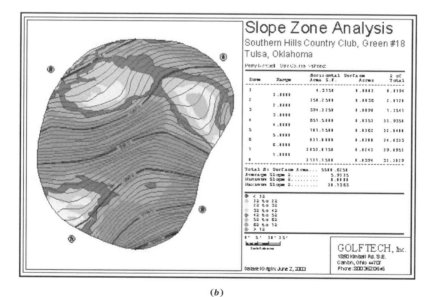

(b)

FIGURE 3-5 (a,b). *LIDAR scanners and GPS are technologies that are currently being used to duplicate greens, to restore old greens to their original contours after reconstruction, and to smooth out older greens so they can have faster green speeds with more pin placements. (Image a courtesy of Scott Pool of Terra Shapers; image b courtesy of Steve Hatfield of GOLFTECH, Inc.)*

23

The main point is that if a golf course has an ideal green speed, then there is a goal to shoot for, which provides a topic of conversation. The pursuit of staying within an ideal green speed can be helpful to the superintendent and his or her staff when engaging in casual conversations or talking about new equipment at budget time. The club's members are far better informed and have gained an appreciation that the 13-foot green speeds they heard about while watching the PGA Tour on the weekend are not appropriate for their greens.

Putting It All Together

In terms of uniformity, an expressed intention of the Stimpmeter was to aid in fair pin placements on contoured greens. It is also apparent that many of the chief architects that aided in the creation and release of the Stimpmeter thought this goal would be best achieved by limiting green speeds on severely contoured greens.

However, they were not naive and they knew that it was possible for the Stimpmeter to be misused. In fact, the dilemma of increasing green speeds on contoured greens was foreseen by Eddie Stimpson; in 1974 he noted, "It may be that greens designed when the average green speed was slower should now be somewhat leveled to take care of the added speed and maintain sufficient choice of pin placement. Large areas that are unusable are a burdensome expense" (Figure 3-5).

Although I do not believe it was anyone's wish that green speed increases would lead to "smoothing out" older classic greens, this has become a practice in order to justify increased pin placements. Moreover, since the release of the Stimpmeter, greens have been built much flatter than in the past to accommodate faster speeds.

I suppose the biggest fear in establishing an ideal green speed is the concern with having to stay within the given range. Therefore, a superintendent should be skilled at communicating why the ideal green speed is or is not met, accordingly, it is time to consider the impact that weather has on green speed.

The Weather: The Known Unknown in the Quest for the Ideal Green Speed

As we know, there are known knowns. There are things we know we know. We also know there are known unknowns. That is to say we know there are some things we do not know. But there are also unknown unknowns, the ones we don't know we don't know.

DONALD RUMSFELD, FEBRUARY 12, 2002,
DEPARTMENT OF DEFENSE NEWS BRIEFING

Controlling the Weather

Humankind has long dreamt about controlling the weather. The ancient Greeks, Romans, and Egyptians prayed and made offerings to the sun and rain gods. In modern Hollywood numerous bad movies have been made depicting diabolical bad guys who dream of controlling the world with their weather machines. However, a weather machine does not exist, and although God may hear all our prayers, often the reply is "No."

Yet, we live in an incredible age of technology that at least allows us to make predictions about the weather. As a result of this increased predictability, there is far less loss of life during hurricanes and tornados than there once was, because we are now allowed more time to prepare for these events.

In our line of work, some of us get genuinely excited about watching the grass grow (especially during a grow-in), so it should come as no surprise to anyone that we also consider the Weather Channel as great TV viewing. In addition, an increasing number of superintendents have computers in their offices, allowing them to monitor the weather continuously. This is a valuable tool that allows superintendents to make better-informed decisions regarding irrigation, pesticide applications, topdressing, crew scheduling, and so forth. However, even with this technology, sometimes the atmosphere does not change in the way we predict it is going to.

It would be of great value to know, within a 6-inch Stimpmeter reading, how rain, humidity, wind, and/or the interaction of all of the weather variables impact green speed. Imagine a database that would allow the superintendent to arrive at the office in the morning, plug in the meteorological conditions of the day before, and receive a response that tells how the green speed has changed. Given this information, the superintendent could make adjustments to that day's cultural practices and stay within the ideal green speed for the course.

Kevin Frank of Michigan State University, Mike Morris, CGCS, and I dreamt of just such a database. Mike took Stimpmeter measurements on two greens at his course every day at approximately 7:00 A.M. and 2:30 P.M. for two consecutive years. Near each green was a weather satellite (Figure 4-1). The daily weather data (broken down into hour increments) and twice daily green speed data were given to Frank, which he put into a statistical program. After countless hours of looking at each individual weather variable, as well as numerous possible interactions, the conclusion was that there was no correlation between changes in the weather and changes that occurred in green speed.

The fact is that weather and its impact on the turfgrass plant, the underlying thatch/mat layer, and the soil is the *known unknown* in the quest for staying within a golf course's ideal green speed. Thus, because we know that we do not know the impact of weather on green speed, the superintendent cannot be blamed when the green speed is periodically above or below the course's ideal green speed. However, there are some interesting findings from studies that a superintendent should know about so that he or she can better inform the club's membership.

Seasonal Variability

I have heard that greens are slower in the summer than in the spring and fall, because the width of the leaf blade is larger in summer. I have also

FIGURE 4-1. *Crystal Downs Country Club, Frankfort, Michigan. A weather satellite was placed near Greens 7 and 12, each having 7:00 A.M. and 2:30 P.M. green speed measurements obtained daily to monitor the impact of the environment on green speed.*

heard that greens are faster in the summer, because the days are longer and the greens are drier. Which is true?

In 1979–1980 a study was performed to evaluate season-long green speed uniformity on nine golf courses in eight states. Stimpmeter measurements were collected weekly on three greens at each golf course. The results included findings that the "courses with the greatest change in green speed occurred on those having transition from cool-season to warm-season turf" and the "two courses with the most consistent green speed occurred in regions where the growing season has less variable weather" (Radko et al., 1981). In other words, in regions with more consistent weather there are more consistent green speeds from day to day.

Another interesting observation can be made regarding mowing height and seasonal changes in green speed, which every superintendent should be aware of. Clark Throssell has been the Director of Research for the GCSAA (Golf Course Superintendents Association of America) since 2001. He earned his master's degree from Pennsylvania State University studying green speed in the early 1980s. He looked at three mowing heights,

[2/32], [3/32], and [6/32] inch on a season-long basis. His data clearly indicates that the highest mowing height (6/32, or 0.187 inch) had the least amount of variability from May to September. Mario Tiziani also did a study that looked at natural variations in putting green speed; he noted that "the faster a green and the better the conditions for turfgrass growth, the greater the green-to-green and day-to-day speed variation" (Tiziani, 1990).

Certainly, the club's members are not going to allow you to raise your mowing heights to 0.187 inch in the name of uniformity. But do not miss out on the strong message within this data. The higher the ideal green speed, the more difficult it is to adhere to it. In other words, faster green speeds are more subject to change due to changes in weather.

Consider the implications of this observation. The Stimpmeter was originally released, in part, to help create more uniform putting conditions from green to green on a given day. Instead, it was more often used to increase green speeds, which, in turn, leads to less uniformity.

Given these conclusions, there is only one way to answer the question regarding seasonal variation that will be useful to you: that is, take daily green speed measurements and immediately enter them into a database and chart them on a graph. This will give you and your membership a better understanding of what is happening on the course.

Diurnal Variability

Most of us have heard golf announcers declare on a Sunday afternoon, "The greens are really getting slick as they continue to dry out." Clearly, the assumption is that greens get faster as the day goes on, but is this true?

Throssell took Stimpmeter measurements at two-hour intervals from 9:00 A.M. to 7:00 P.M. on greens maintained at different mowing heights and under different nitrogen regimes. His finding was that there is "no significant difference in speed measured at 2-hour intervals during the day regardless of nitrogen level or mowing height" (Throssell, 1981).

At Crystal Downs Country Club, we took Stimpmeter measurements at 7:00 A.M. and 2:30 P.M. every day for two straight years. On most occasions the changes in green speed would have been imperceptible to the average golfer. Of particular interest was that on most occasions, the green speed was slower at the 2:30 P.M. measurement than at the 7:00

A.M. measurement. The average change was a 4-inch loss from morning to afternoon in 2001 and a 6-inch loss in green speed from morning to afternoon in 2002. So much for the greens speeding up as the day goes on.

Now consider that there are two opposing forces regarding green speed that are occurring on putting greens every day. The first is that the grass should be growing, how much depending greatly on environmental conditions. The second is that the surface should be getting drier, how dry, again, depending greatly on environmental conditions.

Next, consider the extremes of these opposing forces. Clearly, if it is raining, the surface is not getting drier and, depending on the temperature, the grass is most likely growing. Under these conditions we would expect the greens to get slower. Conversely, if both day and nighttime temperatures are above (or below) optimal growing conditions and it is an extremely dry day with high evapotranspiration rates, we would expect the greens to get faster as the day goes on.

Given these extremes, it appears that diurnal changes in green speed will depend on the area where each particular golf course is located. Clearly, there are regions where the opposing forces of turfgrass growth and drying cancel each other out, which means very little change in green speed throughout the day. The only way to know for certain what the diurnal changes in green speed are at a course is to take an early morning and an afternoon green speed measurement daily. By doing so, the superintendent will not only be able to give the clients some interesting information about their course, but will also be able to compare morning and afternoon changes against the course's cultural practices and determine how they may have influenced green speed.

Rain, Wind, Temperature, and Humidity

Kevin Frank examined the daily Stimpmeter readings from Crystal Downs Country Club from 2001 and 2002 and concluded that there was no correlation between changes in green speed and wind speed, temperature, and humidity. This observation was in agreement with previous work performed in Nebraska that concluded, "Temperature and humidity had no effect on ball-roll distance in either the spring or the summer (Rist and Gaussoin, 1997).

In regard to rain, Frank concluded that when precipitation was greater than 0.5 inch, a drop in green speed should be expected; however, the amount of the loss was not predictable.

Conclusions About Weather and Green Speed

All of the data from studies that have attempted to quantify the impact of weather on green speed is best summed up in the words "We don't know." Even if we had discovered some correlation between green speed and every weather variable at Crystal Downs Country Club, that correlation may have been true for only Crystal Downs.

For example, consider a single weather variable, rain. Assume that a 1-inch rain falls on two neighboring golf courses. The rainfall on these courses could have different effects on their green speeds if they have different root zones (drainage), thatch/mat layer thicknesses (swelling), and possibly even turfgrass species. Even on the same golf course, a

FIGURE 4-2. *Twenty-five years after the release of the Stimpmeter, an increasing number of superintendents are discovering the value of having a personalized green speed record.*

1-inch rain one day could have a different amount of nitrogen than a 1-inch rain on another day, given the presence or lack of lightning, which may also result in differences in green speed. In addition, the duration of the rainfall event would also have to be taken into account. Would we expect a 1-inch rainfall that takes 20 hours to have the same impact on green speed as a 1-inch rainfall that takes 1 hour? The point is that we *know* that weather produces unpredictable outcomes on green speed. Blanket statements such as "The greens get faster later in the day or later in the season" are not accurate.

Clark Throssell noted in his master's thesis, "It was found that variation in speed from season to season or day to day may be greater than variation due to management" (Throssell, 1981). Superintendents who take twice-daily green speed measurements on one or two of their greens will gain an appreciation of how the environment impacts the green speeds on their courses (Figure 4-2).

Putting Green Root Zones

*The varieties of soil that the golfing green-keeper may now
be called on to deal with are very many, and they range
from the lightest of seaside soil to the heaviest of clay.*
HUTCHINSON, 1906

Putting Green Root Zone History

Links are defined as "stretches of rolling, sandy land, especially along a seashore," and it was in this environment on soils of this type that golf originated. As golf grew in popularity, courses moved inland and problems, most notably drainage, arose because of the heavier soils encountered (Hutchinson, 1906). Since really good greens could be found naturally only on sandy soils, it was a common practice to topdress inland greens with sand to make them impervious to wear (Travis, 1901). In the event that the inland native grasses were too coarse and sod was not available, it became essential to construct a good root zone. A 1901 recommendation for putting green construction was to "plough up the surface to a depth of a foot, remove loose materials and fill with a few inches of sand, cover with an inch of loam, then a thin crust of well-rotted manure, another layer of loam (2–3 inches), a dressing of bone dust and lime, cover this with a suggestion of sand, and top off with loam, the surface being raked and finely pulverized" (Travis, 1901). From these early suggestions, a standard 1:1:1 (sand:soil:organic) volume ratio was established in the 1920s–1930s (Hummel, 1993).

Prior to World War II, the problem of compaction in high-clay-content golf greens was not an issue, because traffic was light. After the war, Gen-

33

eral Dwight D. Eisenhower, who had been commander of the allied forces in Europe, was voted 34th president of the United States.

President Eisenhower became famous for playing golf. The servicemen who had followed Eisenhower into battle also followed his lead to the golf course. Thus, after the war, golf became increasingly popular, which resulted in increased traffic and public demand for high-quality turf greens (Beard, 1994). In America, golf went from being a game reserved for the rich to be the common man's game, as illustrated in Table 5-1.

With the increased traffic, it became apparent that soil greens could not hold up, and it was also determined that equal volumes of sand, soil, and peat did not provide adequate permeability (Garman, 1952). Thus, the 1950s became a decade of much research, which ultimately led to the development of United States Golf Association (USGA) Green Section Specifications (Hummell, 1993).

The USGA made its recommendations for putting green construction in 1960 (USGA Green Section Staff, 1960). The recommendations were a departure from the norm, as they advocated the use of a perched water table to ensure a continuous supply of water and a physical analysis of the topsoil mixture with specified micropore and macropore space capacities (Radko, 1973). Since their inception, these recommendations have gone through three revisions, the latest of which occurred in 1993 (Hummell, 1993). However, the basis for the USGA method, which has remained constant, is the recommendation that sand-based root zone mixtures overlay a coarse sand and/or pea gravel layer. The particle-size range of the root zone mixture is the primary property specified within the USGA specifications because of its influence on soil behavior. These specifications include a maximum of particles in the medium and coarse sand size and a minimum of the very coarse and fine-sized particles. This pro-

TABLE 5-1
Forty-two Years of Golf Course Growth

Type of Golf Course	1931	1973
Private	4,448	4,825
Daily fee	700	4,610
Municipal	543	1,436
TOTAL	5,691	10,871

Source: National Golf Foundation

duces a root zone mixture that will maintain a large proportion of macro-pores, which allow rapid water movement and drainage. Since these putting greens have an inherently low capacity for holding plant-available water, different materials (root zone, intermediate layer, and gravel) are stratified, or layered, to increase the ability of the sandy root zone mixture to hold plant-available water.

Besides push-up greens (native soil), there are other types of green construction methods that have been utilized since the release of the USGA recommendations for root zone mix. These include Purr-Wick, Cell-system, and California-style greens, all of which have a root zone that is either entirely or predominantly sand. It is interesting that golf originated on sand centuries ago and, after many years of study, mid-twentieth-century research concluded that high sand content results in the best putting green root zone material.

The Effects of Root Zone on Green Speed

Given that green speeds are not intended for course-to-course compar-isons, would there be any value in knowing whether different root zones produce different green speeds? Clearly, there are numerous instances of multiple types of putting green root zone mixes on a single 18-hole golf course, let alone on a golfing complex with 54+ holes. There are a num-ber of reasons that golf courses have greens with different types of root zones: the addition of holes to an existing nine, the reconstruction of greens, the lengthening of holes by building a new green, and so on. Given these possible variations, the effect of root zone on green speed seems worthy of consideration.

During the summers of 1995 and 1996, I collected a total of 36 Stimp-meter measurements from three putting greens with different root zone mixes at the Hancock Turfgrass Research Center at Michigan State Uni-versity. The putting greens were constructed in 1992 and seeded with Penncross creeping bentgrass in the spring of 1993. The three root zone mixes were an 80:20 (sand: peat v/v) mixture constructed to USGA rec-ommendations, an 80:10:10 (sand: soil: peat volume to volume) mixture built 1 foot deep with subsurface tile drainage, and an undisturbed sandy clay loam (58% sand, 20.5% silt, and 21.5% clay) native soil green. There were three replications of each root zone, which were 40 by 40 feet arranged in a randomized complete block design. All three of the root zone mixes followed identical cultural practice management programs, including the same sand topdressing program.

From the 18 green speed measurements collected in 1995, only 4 resulted in statistical significant differences. In 1996, only 1 of the 18 measurements resulted in statistically significant data.

It is clear that there was no apparent trend indicating that any of the root zones could always be considered faster or slower. In addition, on most days, the three soils could be considered uniform; that is, over the two-year period, all three root zones were within 6 inches of one another 83 percent of the time.

From 1997 to 2000, the same greens were split to include two different nitrogen treatments (3 and 6 pounds N per 1000 square feet per year) and three different potassium treatments (0, 4, and 8 pounds K_2O per 1000 square feet per year). A total of 17 Stimpmeter measurements were taken on the plots from 1998 to 2000. Again, there was no trend suggesting that any of the three putting green root zones, regardless of fertility treatment, resulted in a noticeably faster or slower green speed.

There have been other studies performed that, in part, also looked at the impact of root zone mix on green speed, and data they produced indicates few meaningful differences in green speed resulting from the root zone mix.

Root Zones and Management Practices

It would be impossible to perform a study with every type of putting green root zone mix that would allow us to categorically claim that all root zones produce relatively the same green speeds. Furthermore, if we wanted to set up a study to prove that two root zones resulted in different green speeds, I am relatively certain that we could do so. However, it is probably more realistic to consider root zones relative to management practices and ideal soil moisture ranges for a golf course putting green.

In my study, all three greens were topdressed with sand every two to three weeks throughout the growing season, depending on growth. I managed the different root zones with the same topdressing schedule and material. In this situation, it certainly makes sense that there would be very little difference between the impacts of the different root zones on green speed. After all, the friction between the golf ball and the surface of the green is what determines the green speed. If all greens are subject to the same frequent sand topdressing treatment (and other cultural practices), we can also assume that they would have relatively the same amount of thatch. If the thatch is of the same thickness, the surface hardness should be relatively the same; thus, the ball should sink (unperceivably) to the same depth, resulting in the same relative green speed.

Soil moisture must also be taken into account. You may recall that an ideal soil is composed of approximately 50 percent solids and 50 percent pore space by volume. When half the pore spaces are filled with water and the rest with air (i.e., 50 percent solid, 25 percent water, and 25 percent air), the soil is considered ideal for plant growth. Maintaining a soil at these percentages for an extended period of time is nearly impossible in the field. Clearly, given the same amounts of irrigation, if the 50 percent solid portion of the soil is sand, there will be fewer water-filled pores than if the solid fragment is clay.

Now consider the ideal soil moisture range for a golf course green. On almost every green, nearly every morning a nonscientific yet extremely useful soil moisture reading is taken with a device known as a cup-cutter. With a minimum degree of force, the cup-cutter should be able to enter the root zone to a depth of approximately 8 inches. The core that is removed by the cup-cutter should remain virtually intact when removed from the root zone. If these two criteria are *not* met in the core produced by the cup-cutter, soil moisture is most often adjusted through irrigation. However, irrigation should never result in water pooling in the cup. The more experienced an individual becomes at taking morning cup-cutter moisture readings on a given set of greens, the better that person seems to get at applying the proper irrigation.

Before courses had their own weather stations and evapotranspiration (ET) was factored in as part of a computerized equation for nightly irrigation, there were always daily attempts by the golf course superintendent and staff to provide the best playing conditions for the golfer. Generally, if the superintendent is managing greens constructed with different root zones the same way, then it is safe to expect that the different root zones will result in the same green speed (within 6 inches) most of the time. The most important variable in this treatment is irrigation, which is adjusted appropriately for each green every night. Sometimes there are large rainfalls that cause the course to be shut down for a period of time. These natural events may result in thatch swelling. Under such circumstances, it would be logical to theorize that greens constructed with different root zones could have different green speeds for a short period of time. However, given time to drain, the greens should return to having relatively the same green speeds with proper management.

Turfgrass Species and Green Speed

*Bent grasses in this climate do better when cut very close
throughout the season. Bluegrass, redtop, and fescue thrive
better when not cut so close, but should be cut just as
often; naturally they make slower greens.*

**W. S. HARBAN, GREENS KEEPER AT COLUMBIA
COUNTRY CLUB, CHEVY CHASE, MARYLAND, 1922**

The Birth of Golf Turf Research

In 1908, during the construction of the National Links on Long Island, serious problems were encountered in attempts to grow turf on old sand
dunes. This dilemma led Charles B. MacDonald to apply for assistance
from the Department of Agriculture. In studying turf problems at the National Links, the Department scientists quickly realized that the existing
knowledge about turf was far from adequate and that experimental investigations were necessary. At that time no funds were available for
turfgrass research; however, a cooperative effort was undertaken by several golf clubs and turfgrass investigations were made under the guidance
of C. V. Piper and R. A. Oakley, USDA.

Articles on turfgrass written by Piper and Oakley began to appear in
1913, and although they were seen as immensely helpful, the needs of
the golf clubs for information and advice increased enormously. In the
spring of 1915, the United States Golf Association (USGA) requested help
from the Department of Agriculture in solving problems associated with
greenkeeping. At that time, the USGA pointed out that about $10 million
per year was being spent on the establishment and maintenance of turf
by golf clubs. It was believed that half of the money was being wasted

39

because of ignorance. As a result, turf research was initiated at the turf gardens at the Arlington Experiment Farm in Virginia in the spring of 1916 (Monteith, 1928).

The best-suited turfgrass for a putting surface had been debated for years. The following observation was made at that time, which still holds true today:

> Many factors must be considered before deciding as to the best grass for a putting green. Some of these are biological and have to do with the growing of grass, such as resistance to trampling, ability to withstand extremes of heat or cold, response to the soil in which it must grow, disease resistance and many others. The ultimate aim in developing putting greens is to provide an area on which a ball may be rolled with the greatest possible accuracy and a surface which will remain in good condition throughout as long a season as possible. It is now generally recognized that the surface of the soil, like the slate under the billiard table cloth, is the part that largely determines the accuracy of the green. The speed, uniformity, and other minor characteristics of a putting green may depend chiefly on the quality of the grass growing upon it (Monteith, 1929).

Certainly, it should come as no surprise that some of the earliest research on turfgrass was to identify the most suitable grasses for the putting surface. Turfgrasses planted for early putting green experiments included various species of bentgrass, Bermudagrass, fescue, ryegrass, Manila grass, Buffalograss, couch grass, Kentucky bluegrass, and annual bluegrass.

Among the considerations for a good putting green turf was the need for speed. R. A. Oakley noted in 1924 that red fescues could not tolerate the close cutting height required for the fast greens that the players demanded on their putting surfaces. Thus, there was a connection made between mowing height and green speed, and since fescue could not tolerate mowing heights that gave golfers the desired speeds they required, it was determined that it did not make a good putting surface (Oakley, 1926).

Early Perceptions of Green Speed on Various Turfgrass Species

Bentgrass species and how they were propagated constituted another cause of debate in the 1920s and 1930s. It was commonly believed that bentgrasses established by the stolon method and those established by seed resulted in different green speeds. Some believed that "stolons should not be planted on any slopes with more than a 2-percent grade, for the reason that a ball could not be stopped on a stolon planted turf when the grade exceeded 2 percent (Grau, 1933).

To address this belief, Fred Grau conducted the first green speed studies at the turf gardens at the Arlington Experiment Farm, Arlington, Virginia, in 1932. Grau did not have a Stimpmeter (it would not be invented for another five years), but he did have the Arnott mechanical putter.

The mechanical putter was invented by R. F. Arnott of the Upper Montclair (New Jersey) Country Club, and in 1928, Arnott gave his invention to the USGA. The mechanical putter was invented with the intention to measure differences in green speed that might be found among various putting green grasses.

The Arnott mechanical putter was essentially a pendulum mounted on a tripod. At the base of the pendulum was a putter blade. Testing with the machine was described by Monteith as follows:

> To operate the machine the tripod is set with the top level and at the desired height. The pendulum is allowed to swing free, and when it has come to rest a ball is placed just in front of the center of the blade. The spring is adjusted and the pendulum is drawn back and held by means of a hook attached to the back leg of the tripod. A slight touch releases this hook and the pendulum swings forward and strikes the ball. In making the tests the machine is set up at the edge of the plot and a ball is repeatedly putted from the same position. The average distance of several (usually five) putts is taken as the distance for that setting on that particular grass. After several repetitions of the above, both upgrade and downgrade on the different grasses, there is something more than mere personal opinions on which to base a judgment as to the relative putting qualities, particularly that of speed, of the various grasses (Monteith, 1929).

Initially included in Grau's green speed experiment were "all the popular types of bentgrass that are used on American golf courses," as well as fescue and annual bluegrass. However, because of summer injuries, the fescue and the *Poa annua* were eliminated from the experiment. The study proceeded with a total of eight bentgrasses, three of which were planted from seed and five that were established by stolons. It was believed at the time that *Poa annua* died from summer heat stress. We know today this is not true, but was most likely a disease. Fescue is no longer used on putting greens in the United States.

After performing 13 tests throughout the season with the Arnott mechanical putter, Grau concluded, "[The] tests clearly indicate that the variety and type of grass exert no such influence on the speed of turf as they are popularly supposed to have." Grau further noted,

Changes in the height at which the mower is set, and changes in topdressing, watering, raking or brushing, and fertilizing, and changes in other maintenance practices largely determine the speed of the putting surface.

The tests clearly show, however, that if grasses are properly cared for they do not present as much variation in speed of putting as is so commonly attributed to them (Grau, 1933).

Current Research with Putting Green Turf Species

Today, with genetic breeding programs prevalent, there are far more than the eight most common bentgrasses that Grau had to deal with in 1932. Fortunately, the National Turfgrass Evaluation Program (NTEP) has allowed research to continue regarding turfgrass species and green speed. NTEP is a cooperative effort between the nonprofit National Turfgrass Federation, Inc., and the United States Department of Agriculture.

In 1997, a joint effort between the USGA, the Golf Course Superintendents Association of America (GCSAA), and NTEP agreed to revitalize on-site testing of putting green turfgrass cultivars. Sixteen trial sites were located on golf courses in northern locations for bentgrass, in southern locations for Bermudagrass, and in the transition zone for both species. Eighteen different cultivars of bentgrass were seeded at their prospective sites in 1997, and seven of the most commonly utilized Bermudagrasses were propagated at their prospective sites in 1998. Data collection continued at the sites through 2001. During this time period, numerous Stimpmeter measurements were recorded at the sites. The result was that there were a few, but no meaningful differences in green speed attributed to the different bentgrasses or Bermudagrasses in the studies. Results of NTEP tests can be found at *www.ntep.org*.

Over the years, numerous studies have been performed on putting green turfgrass cultivars to determine if there are any meaningful differences in their effects on green speed. One that I found interesting was performed by Phil Busey and Susan Boyer, who obtained green speed measurements on seven hybrid Bermudagrasses and five *Cynodon transvallensis* genotypes (Busey, 2001). Busey reported that the African Bermudagrasses were as much as 9 inches slower than the slowest hybrids. However, most of the African Bermudagrasses died in the summer and thus could not be considered viable putting green turfgrasses. Among the hybrids in this study, the fastest was Quality Dwarf, which had a Stimpmeter reading of 8 feet 6 inches, and the slowest hybrid was

TifEagle, which had a green speed of 8 feet 4 inches. Although these differences are statistically significant, they are too small to be of any practical use.

Busey and Boyer also took on the contention that cool-season grasses are faster than warm-season grasses. They had an opportunity to test this legendary assumption with Penneagle bentgrass that was persistently growing in patches in a Bermudagrass green. The results were that the Bermudagrass averaged 9 feet on the Stimpmeter and the bentgrass averaged 8 feet 7 inches. Again, the results were statistically significant, but of no practical difference.

Conclusions About Turfgrass Species

The initial green speed experiments performed on turfgrass were designed to determine differences in green speed associated with different putting green grasses and the way those grasses were established. It was concluded in 1932, and has been corroborated ever since, that when grasses are treated with the same cultural practices (and live), there are no meaningful consistent differences in green speed among them.

When selecting a species for a putting green surface, a cultivar should be chosen that does best in a specified region. Furthermore, the appropriate recommended cultural practices should be followed to give the particular species the best chance to recuperate and thrive.

In regard to their relation to green speed, some of the newer cultivars of Bermudagrass and bentgrass are reported to tolerate slightly lower mowing heights than their predecessors. "Tifgreen Bermudagrass should be maintained in a range of $10/64$ inch to $7/32$ inch. Tifdwarf, on the other hand, should ideally be maintained in a range from $\frac{1}{8}$ to $\frac{3}{16}$ inch (White, 1985). Certainly, tighter mowing heights lead to faster green speeds, but there is always a point of diminishing returns. The next chapter discusses mowing height and its effect on green speed.

Mowing Height

*Putting greens must have turf of fine texture and of
uniform surface. To accomplish this, close cutting is
necessary and, with the modern putting green mower, it is
possible literally to shave the grass down to the very
surface of the ground. Because of the urge of the players
for fast greens, the greenkeeper is inclined almost
unknowingly to cut the grass exceedingly close.*
OAKLEY, 1926

It is clear that golfer demands for fast putting surfaces and mowing height have been closely linked for a long time. Certainly, if there is one aspect of putting green management that a golfer understands, it is that lower mowing heights lead to faster green speeds. However, as the cliché goes, "A little knowledge is a dangerous thing." The majority of golfers have little if any understanding of the impact that bedknife thickness, triplex versus walk-behind mowers, walk-behind drum-style versus floating head, type of roller, and grommers have on green speed. In addition, the same golfer who demands faster green speeds may also complain because the greens have moss or the turf seems thin. Considering that an objective of this book is to aid the superintendent in becoming the authority on green speed at his or her golf course, it is pertinent that the superintendent be knowledgeable about the history of mowing heights on the putting surface. Therefore, a brief history of putting green mowing height is provided prior to the discussion of the effects of mowing height on green speed.

History of Putting Green Mowing Height

In 1929, Sir Robert Greig wrote, "If it had been necessary to cut and roll putting greens there would have been no golf until the mowing machine was invented about 50 years ago, as even the most skilled scytheman could not have mown a putting green" (Anonymous, 1929b). If putting greens were not cut and rolled, then just how were they maintained? "There are greens on which the rabbits are the chief, and almost the only, greenkeepers. The rabbits crop the grass short and produce an admirable quality of springy turf. I do not suppose any other greens are kept up to an equal degree of excellence with so little expense in wages of green-keepers as these, and all because the rabbits do so much of the work, without payment" (Hutchinson, 1906). And so it was that a common duty of the early greenkeepers was to brush away rabbit pellets from the putting greens. Thus, early on a trend was set: The rabbits got the credit, the membership kept the money, and the greenkeeper got the rest.

The rabbit putting green mower system was adequate until the rubber-cored ball replaced the gutta ball around the dawn of the twentieth century. The rubber-cored ball was livelier than the gutta ball, demanding smoother putting surfaces than mowing by rabbits could provide (Mackie, 1929).

In 1922, the United States Golf Association (USGA) interviewed 15 golf course superintendents about putting green maintenance. In that discussion, many remarked about the need for good speed on their greens and noted that they "cut very close throughout the season" and that "the mower knifes are pushed down to the lowest notch" (Harban et al., 1922). However, one of them, A. J. Hood of the Detroit Golf Club, gave the first measured mowing height I have come across, when he wrote, "At the beginning of the season we set our blades up somewhat higher, and gradually work them down to about three-eighths" (Harban et al., 1922). I must admit that ⅜ inch is a little tighter than I would have expected in 1922, but that mowing height was soon perceived as being too high.

During the 1920s, many new types of power mowers for putting greens were released, and mowing heights became tighter. The tighter mowing heights became evident when, in 1930, Howard Sprague of the New Jersey experiment station wrote, "The height at which turf should be cut depends on two factors; namely the use made of the turf, and the ability of the turf plants to tolerate close mowing. Turf plants which are suitable for fine turf must be capable of making vigorous growth when cut to a length of *three-sixteenths inch each day during growing weather*" (Sprague and Evaul, 1930). To prove that Sprague's comments were not erroneous, Grau noted about his putting green plots, "Grasses in this series of plots are kept in as good condition as modern cultural methods will permit. They are all cut at the same time with the mower set to cut at $3/16$ of an inch" (Grau 1933). From these comments it is clear that $3/16$ inch was as tight as a green could be maintained at that time.

In a 1947 USGA mowing survey report, approximately 25 percent of the responding golf courses reported mowing their greens at a $3/16$-inch height of cut, roughly 50 percent mowed them at $1/4$ inch, and the rest mowed them at $5/16$ inch or higher (Anonymous, 1947) (See Table 7-1).

As a result of this survey, it was determined that the "best" height of cut for good putting surfaces is in the range of $3/16$- to $1/4$-inch. Twenty-six years later, James Beard wrote in his book *Turfgrass Science and Culture* that bentgrass tolerated "continuous, close mowing at heights as low as 0.2 in" (Beard, 1973). We can infer from the observations by Sprague in 1930, the USGA 1947 survey, and the Beard text in 1973 that putting green mowing heights, and the recommended daily frequency of cut, changed very little between 1930 and 1973. What is also clear is that the $3/16$-inch mowing height was as tight as greens were cut from the late 1920s into the early 1970s.

Given this fact, we might similarly expect that the *average* green speed would have changed little over this period. Indeed, the only individual known to have a Stimpmeter during this time was Eddie Stimpson. Stimpson wrote two articles in his lifetime, the first in 1937 and the second in 1974. In the first article, he mentions six Stimpmeter measurements that he made in 1937. The average green speed derived from those six measurements was 27 inches (remember, this is *not* the same Stimpmeter we

TABLE 7-1

*Height of Cut on Putting Greens
Reported from 27 States in a
1947 USGA Mowing Survey*

	$3/16''$	$1/4''$	$5/16''$
Spring	18	31	17
Summer	25	26	37
Fall	23	35	18

use today). In his 1974 article, Stimpson listed seven Stimpmeter measurements that he obtained from 1946 through to 1973, and the average green speed at the seven sites was also 27 inches (Table 7-2). Given that these are the only green speed measurements I am aware of that were made during this period, it appears that green speed changed very little from 1937 to 1973. Unfortunately, no one ever correlated the differences in green speed measurements between the original wooden Stimpmeter and the current aluminum model. I can't help but wonder how close the 27 inch average that Stimpson's readings produced is to the 6 foot 6 inch average that resulted from the USGA's 1500 measurements in 1976–1977.

Soon after Eddie Stimpson's second article in 1974, two events occurred that would dramatically change green speed. The first was that machining equipment was refined to the degree that thinner bedknives

TABLE 7-2

Stimpmeter Measurements Reported by Eddie Stimpson in His 1937 and 1974 Articles

1937 Stimpmeter Readings	Ball Roll Distance (inches)	1946–1973 Stimpmeter Readings	Ball Roll Distance (inches)
Brae Burn (shortest annual distance)	19	1946 Charles River, Massachusetts State Amateur	22
Brae Burn (longest annual distance)	36	1963 Brae Burn, New England Amateur	25
Brae Burn (shaded moist green)	27	1963 The Country Club, The United States Open	32
Brae Burn (sun-dried green)	36	1965 Pleasant Valley, Carling Open	19
Country Club in Brookline (during the Cup Tournament)	24	1965 Woodland, Massachusetts Amateur	26
Woollaston Golf Club Boston 4 Ball League Match	18	1973 The Country Club, Walker Cup	32
		1973 Onwentsia, USGA Senior Amateur	31
Average Green Speed 1937	27	**Average Green Speed 1946–1973**	27

became mass producible, which in turn allowed for tighter mowing on putting surfaces. Second, the USGA released the Stimpmeter, making green speed quantifiable on any golf course for the first time in history. After nearly 50 years of very little change in mowing heights and green speeds, golf entered a phase of dramatic change on the putting surface not seen since the replacement of the rabbit for the mower.

The Law of Diminishing Returns

Since the release of the Stimpmeter in 1978, a number of studies have looked at the impact of mowing height on green speed. Before considering these studies, it may be helpful to review the law of diminishing returns. Webster's defines *diminishing returns* as "the proportionately smaller increase in productivity observed after a certain point in the increase of capital, labor, etc." Thus, the point of diminishing returns is the point where increasing input is no longer validated by the outcome. In regard to green speed, I apply the term to any management practice that results in a change in green speed of less than 6 inches as measured with a Stimpmeter. However, there should be one amendment: "unless the goal is to change the green speed on a certain putting surface to make it uniform (within 6 inches) with the other putting surfaces on the golf course," which is most currently practiced during major tournaments. In Table 7-3 are my interpretations from several of the studies on mowing height and green speed that have been done since the release of the Stimpmeter. The primary investigator(s) and the year results were published are included next to their findings. The one clear observation that can be drawn from the studies is that lowering the mowing height does increase green speed. However, it is also evident that there is no known green speed increase that results from an incremental drop in mowing height. In other words, it would have been convenient if a $1/32$-inch drop in the mowing height always produced a known increase in green speed, such as 1 foot, but, unfortunately, that is not the case. However, I would like to make some generalities regarding the mowing height/green speed studies that are based on evaluation of the data.

When mowing height drops $1/32$ inch (0.031) from $3/16$ inch (0.187) down to $5/32$ inch (0.156), the corresponding increase in green speed should be within the range of 1 foot to 6 inches, in most cases closer to 1 foot. The next $1/32$-inch incremental drop in mowing height is from $5/32$

TABLE 7-3
Green Speed–Mowing Height Studies

Researcher/Year	Results
Throssell, 1981	Research conducted on mowing heights of $2/32$ (0.06), $3/32$ (0.09), and $6/32$ (0.187) inches resulted in an average change in green speed of 6 to 8 inches for every $1/32$-inch change in mowing height.
Langlois, 1985	An increase of 2 feet occurred when mowing height was lowered from 0.187 to 0.125 inches. However, only a 4-inch increase occurred when mowing height was lowered from 0.125 to 0.09 inch.
Nus and Haupt, 1989	Research was conducted on the mowing heights of $3/32$ (0.09) and $6/32$ (0.187) inches resulting in an average difference in green speed of 2 feet 3 inches.
Salaiz, Horst, and Shearman 1995	An increase in green speed of approximately 1 foot occurred as mowing height was lowered from 0.189 to 0.125 inch.
Kussow, 1998	Mowing heights in the study were 0.234, 0.156, and 0.109 inch. Green speed increased by 1 foot 9 inches, with the drop from 0.234 to 0.156 inch, and by 1 foot 1 inch with the drop from 0.156 to 0.109 inch.
Yelverton, 1998	Research considered the mowing heights of 0.189, 0.157, and 0.125 inch. As mowing height increased, putting green speed slowed by approximately 1 foot for each $1/32$ inch (0.031) increase in mowing height.

inch down to $1/8$ inch (0.125), and the data suggests that it will similarly result in a change in green speed between 1 foot and 6 inches. Reduction of the mowing height an additional $1/32$ inch to $3/32$ inch (0.094) will result in an increase of green speed of approximately 4 inches. Given that a golfer cannot detect a difference in green speed of 6 inches or less, this implies that incremental drops of $1/32$ inch (or less) below a mowing height of 0.125 inch have hit the point of diminishing returns. In other words, mowing heights between 0.125 inch and 0.09 inch will most likely result in no noticeable change in green speed. This law of diminishing returns with mowing height is illustrated in Figure 7-1.

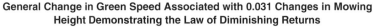

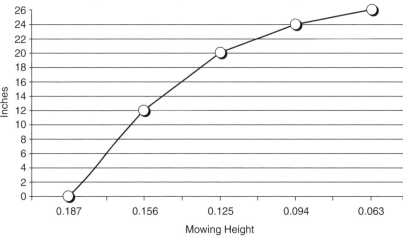

General Change in Green Speed Associated with 0.031 Changes in Mowing Height Demonstrating the Law of Diminishing Returns

FIGURE 7-1.

It is my understanding that modern-day mowing equipment gives the golf course superintendent the possibility of mowing as low as 0.0625 inch (Happ, 2003). I have also read that a mowing height of 0.0625 inch should be considered only if the members prescribe to the motto, "Green is good, fast is better," money is not limited, if the grass is a newer variety of bentgrass in the north or an ultradwarf in the south, and if the superintendent has his resume up to date. Clark Throssell mowed Penncross, Penneagle, and Seaside bentgrass greens at a 0.06 inch mowing height as part of his master's thesis, but it seems apparent that the surface was as much a combination of thatch and moss as grass. Averaged over the three species, moss had infested 46 percent of the plots. In addition, a mowing height of 0.06 inch is no guarantee that the green speed will be any faster (> 6 inches) than that of greens managed at a mowing height of 0.120 inch. Such a possibility is discussed further in the following section on mower types.

It is important to keep in mind that my comments concerning mowing height and green speed, as presented in Figure 7-1, are my general interpretations. Although they are based on examining the scientific data, they are *not* concrete facts. My point was to demonstrate the law of diminishing returns to give the superintendent a valuable fact to consider. I periodically hear of golf courses dropping their mowing height from

0.120 inch to 0.110 inch to increase green speed, and the data strongly suggests that the objective is not being achieved. From an agronomic perspective there are numerous advantages of mowing at the highest possible mowing height. Mowing bentgrass putting greens at "0.125 inch or less has a high biological cost" that includes decreased traffic tolerance, reductions in turf density, increased algae growth, and a decrease in root weight by "nearly 100 percent" in the hottest part of the season (Kussow, 1998). "Instead of entering into the contest to see how low greens can be cut, the contest should be to find out how high turf can be cut without serious complaints" (Knoop, 2000). The best way to accomplish that is to determine a course's ideal green speed and consider the law of diminishing returns in relation to your mowing height.

An important question arises: Why weren't the results of the mowing height–green speed studies more similar? There are two good explanations: (1) There was different mowing equipment at each site, and (2) the cultural practices (and certainly the climatic factors) were not the same at the different locations. These two points require additional investigation.

Mower Height versus Height of Cut

Just as Directive 1 in the Stimpmeter instruction booklet states that Stimpmeter readings are "not intended for course comparisons," mowing heights should likewise not be used for course comparisons. The reason is that all mowers set at the same height do not result in the same height of cut. Furthermore, it is necessary to define the terms *mowing height* and *height of cut*. Although it is true that these terms are generally used interchangeably, it is important to clarify the differences as used in this book.

The term *mowing height* refers to the distance between the bedknife and the reel as set in the shop, and *height of cut* is the length of the verdure that remains after mowing. It would be ideal if the mowing height and the height of cut were the same, but this is not the case. Different mower types, heads, bedknives, rollers, and groomers can have a significant impact on increasing the difference between the mowing height and the height of cut (Figure 7-2).

The golfer will always assume that lowering the mowing height will lead to a noticeable increase in green speed. However, as previously discussed, this is not always the case, because of the law of diminishing re-

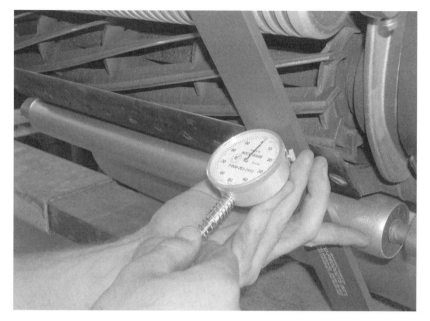

FIGURE 7-2. *Modern technology offers a superintendent the precision equipment necessary to achieve low mowing heights on a putting surface.*

turns. Golfers also expect that if green speeds are faster at course A than at course B, then course A would have to have the lower mowing height. This is also not true. The inability of a superintendent to communicate the intricacies of mowing height and the actual height of cut to the more influential club members can cause unnecessary complications for that golf course superintendent.

Illustrating this point is a 1965 query that reads as follows: "The golf course superintendent at our club tells us that he mows greens at ¼ inch. At a neighboring club, the greens are mowed at ⁵/₁₆ inch, yet their greens seem faster than ours. Can you explain?" (USGA Green Section Staff, 1965). Three points worthy of consideration form the query:

1. The member doubts his superintendent's word regarding the course mowing height. This is evident from the words "tells us."

2. The member unequivocally believes his source of information about the neighboring course, as suggested by the words, "are mowed."

3. The member thinks mowing height is the end-all in green speed and therefore cannot understand how greens mowed at a greater

mowing height can result in faster green speeds than greens mowed at a lower mowing height.

To bring the question up to date, suppose one green is mowed at 0.157 inch and the other at 0.120 inch. Furthermore, assume that all other management practices are the same. Is it possible that the green maintained at the 0.157-inch mowing height could result in green speeds as fast as, or faster, than those of the green maintained at the 0.120-inch mowing height? The answer is yes, given that they are mowed with different mowers.

Mower Types

When the triplex mower was first introduced for the putting surface, it was noted that it had to be set at least 1/16 inch lower than walk-behind mowers to achieve the same height of cut (Anonymous, 1971). From the mowing height–green speed studies performed, we can generalize that a change in mowing height of 1/16 (0.06) inch can produce a green speed difference of as much as 2 feet, so this setting would obviously result in a noticeable difference. It has also been reported that it is possible for two identical putting green mowers to be set at the same mowing height and yet have the true height of cut vary by approximately 1/8 of an inch just because of differences in bedknife thickness (Hoos and Faust, 1979).

Mower Type–Green Speed Study

During the summer of 2002, three golf course superintendents in three different regions in the United States investigated the impact of mower type on their putting green speeds. At all three locations, the superintendents initiated the research by establishing plots to mow with their triplex and walk-behind mowers (Figure 7-3). In addition, the same individual set the mowing height at each location. All mowers at all three locations had Wiley rollers in the front and smooth rollers in the rear. As in any valid research, there were three replications of each treatment.

After mowing, green speed measurements were obtained with a Stimpmeter in a manner consistent with USGA specifications. At all three locations the study ran at least two weeks.

FIGURE 7-3. *Even if mowing height, rollers, and bedknife thickness are the same, walk-behind mowers generally result in faster green speeds than triplex mowers.*

Superintendent Chris Sykes and his assistant, Jason Anderson, at Chero-kee Country Club in Knoxville, Tennessee, performed research on their Crenshaw creeping bentgrass nursery green. Chris used a John Deere 2500 triplex and three different walk-behind mowers. Two of the walk-behinds were John Deere 220A drum-type mowers, one of which was equipped with a groomer. The remaining walk-behind was a Toro 500 with a floating head. All mowers were set at a 0.120-inch mowing height.

Tom Baty, superintendent at Bend Golf and Country Club in Bend, Oregon, performed research on a *Poa annua* nursery green. The triplex mower was a Jacobson GreenKing V, and the walk-behind was a John Deere 220 drum-style mower. Both mowers were set at a 0.140-inch mowing height.

Superintendent Rob Buege and assistant Greg Laue, Tara Golf and Country Club in Bradenton, Florida, performed their research on the club's Tifdwarf practice putting green. The triplex mower was a Toro Greensmaster 3000, and the walk-behind was a John Deere 220 drum-style mower. In preparation for the study, the reels were ground, bed-knives faced, and both mowers set at a 0.125-inch mowing height.

Furthermore, after mowing plots and collecting data for two weeks, research continued at both Bend and Tara Country Clubs, but with an added dimension. At both locations, mowing treatments continued, but all plots were rolled three days a week with a True-Surface vibratory roller. The objective of this study was to determine if other cultural practices (in this case, lightweight rolling) would exacerbate green speed differences produced by the different mower treatments.

Results from the mowing height–green speed measurements averaged over the two-week period are reported in Table 7-4. At all three locations the triplex mowers averaged lower green speeds as compared with walk-behind mowers, though not all differences were significant. However, there were dramatic differences from site to site.

The site showing the greatest difference in green speed due to differences in mower types was the Crenshaw creeping bentgrass nursery green in Knoxville, Tennessee. At that site, plots mowed with the John Deere drum-style walk-behind mower averaged a 1-foot increase in green

TABLE 7-4

The Effect of Mower Type on Green Speed Reported in Feet and Inches from Three Country Clubs, 2003

Mower Treatment	Knoxville, Tennessee Penncross, MH 0.12 inch	Bend, Oregon *Poa annua*, MH 0.14 inch	Bradenton, Florida Tifdwarf, MH 0.125 inch
Triplex	9'1"b	9'2"b	9'3"
Walk-behind drum-type	10'1"a	9'8"a	9'5"
Walk-behind with groomer	10'3"a	—	—
Walk-behind with floating head	9'7"ab		
	*	**	NS

Notes:
MH = mowing height.
* *means significant within a probability of 0.05.*
** *means significant within a probability of 0.01.*
NS = Not Significant.
LSD = Least Significant Difference.
Means in columns followed by the same letter are not significantly different at the 0.05 level using the LSD mean separation test.

speed as compared with those mowed with the triplex mower. No mean-ingful difference in green speed was found between plots mowed with the John Deere drum-style mowers with or without the groomer. The Toro walk-behind with floating head resulted in an average green speed directly between the average green speeds of the triplex and the drum-style walk-behind mower.

As I mentioned earlier, a green maintained at a mowing height of 0.06 inch is no guarantee that the green speed will be any faster (>6 inch) than a green managed at a mowing height of 0.12 inch. I know that seems impossible, but consider Chris Sykes's data regarding drum-type and flex mower walk-behinds coupled with the law of diminishing returns. It is my understanding that on contoured putting surfaces, to achieve a mow-ing height as low as 0.06 inch, a floating head is recommended to pre-vent scalping. If this true, and a mowing height of 0.12 inch can be achieved with a drum-type mower, Syke's data, coupled with the law of diminishing returns, indicates that there would be no *noticeable* differ-ences between the two mowing heights.

So how does Chris utilize this data? Chris Sykes uses the John Deere walk-behinds two months of the year to verticut and has always theorized that drum-type walk-behinds put the entire weight of the machine on the cutting head. For this reason he sets the mowing height on his drum-type walk-behind at 0.14 inch, whereas his Toro floating-head walk-behinds are normally set at a 0.12 inch mowing height.

Results of the research on green speed and mower types were not as severe at the other golf courses that participated in the study. In Bend, Oregon, the *Poa annua* plots mowed with the drum-style walk-behind mower averaged 6-inch longer ball roll as compared with plots mowed with the triplex. As stated previously, after two weeks superintendent Baty initiated lightweight rolling in his mower-type study. When the *Poa annua* plots were rolled, the average difference in green speed between mower types increased, as plots mowed with the walk-behind averaged 8 inches faster than plots mowed with the triplex on the day of rolling and the day after rolling had been applied (Table 7-5).

Tom Baty stated that when he originally arrived at his course, the "mowing height was 0.11. That seemed a bit tight to me, but I figured that must be how they mow them here." However, Tom also had moss on his greens, so he slowly raised the cutting height and started rolling three days per week. "Now my cutting height is 0.14, but I roll every other day to keep green speeds up and my members happy." This is a

TABLE 7-5

The Effect of Rolling Greens Mowed with Two Different
Mower Types on Green Speed, Reported in Feet and Inches
at Two Country Clubs, 2003

Mower Treatment	Bend Golf and Country Club, Bend, Oregon *Poa annua* at a 0.14 inch Cutting Height		Tara Golf and Country Club, Bradenton, Florida Tifdwarf at a 0.125 inch Cutting Height	
	Day Both Treatments Rolled After Mowing	Day After Both Treatments Rolled After Mowing	Day Both Treatments Rolled After Mowing	Day After Both Treatments Rolled After Mowing
Triplex	10'0"	9'6"	9'5"	8'9"
Walk-behind	10'8"	10'2"	10'1"	9'1"
	***	**	*	NS

*, **, and *** Significant at the 0.05, 0.01, and 0.001 probability levels, respectively.
NS, nonsignificant at the 0.05 probability level.

case of a superintendent successfully addressing the law of diminishing returns as well as the aesthetics and health of his greens.

On the Tifdwarf nursery green at Tara Golf and Country Club, there were no statistical differences in green speed between mower treatments after two weeks of mowing. However, when the cultural practice of rolling was added to the Tifdwarf green, plots mowed with the walk-behind mower averaged 8 inches faster than plots mowed with the triplex mower on the day rolling was applied. The day after rolling, the difference in green speed between mowers was no longer significant.

Initially, differences in green speed between mower types was not as dramatic on the Tifdwarf test plots, as compared with the two sites with cool-season grasses. However, when the cultural practice of lightweight rolling was added, the differences became significant. Assistant Greg Laue noted, "The data generated at Tara illustrates that green speed management must take into account all cultural management practices utilized on the putting surface."

Recall the question posed earlier, Why weren't the results of the mowing height–green speed studies more similar? Two possible explanations were given: (1) The cultural practices (and certainly the climatic factors) were not the same at the different locations, and (2) the mowing equipment was different. Results from the studies performed at the three golf courses considered here clearly demonstrate that because of differences in mowing equipment, identical mowing heights cannot be expected to result in similar green speed changes. Moreover, the use of various cultural practices can exacerbate the inherent differences between the mowing equipment even further.

It is unfortunate that using the same mowing height will not always result in the same height of cut. It is also unfortunate that there is no magical incremental change in mowing height that will result in a known change in green speed. What is there to learn from this? Most important, superintendents should always consider the law of diminishing returns in regard to their mowing height. Superintendents who want to find the point of diminishing returns on their golf courses can use their nursery or practice greens as did the superintendents mentioned earlier. Plots can be maintained with the same piece of equipment at mowing heights of 0.14, 0.13, 0.12, and 0.01 inch for several weeks, and the data collected and shared with the green committee members or owners. The result will be a clear understanding of how mowing height affects golf course putting greens, a point of diminishing returns will be found, and the superintendent will enhance his or her reputation with the membership. The best way to know what is going on is to create what is going on.

Double Cutting

Double cutting is the practice of mowing the same green twice on the same day. In many cases the two mowings are at 90-degree angles of each another. Some golf courses perform this cultural practice daily throughout the playing season, and even more utilize the practice during club championships. Still others raise the mowing height slightly during periods of stress, but double cut to retain green speeds.

Over the years, there has been some intriguing information generated by several double cutting studies. Clark Throssell performed a study that was unique because it considered three different varieties of bentgrass (Penncross, Penneagle, and Seaside) mowed at three different mowing heights (0.187, 0.094, and 0.063 inch). Results from his work indicated that (1) there was no difference in green speed attributed to the bent-grass varieties, and (2) as mowing height decreased, so too did the increase in green speed attributed to the second mowing. Throssell attributed increases in green speed following the double cut to the "removal of leaves not mowed during the first mowing" (Throssell, 1981). Numerous papers have stated that as mowing heights decrease, the plant texture decreases, as does the turfgrass density. If this is true, then it seems logical that grass maintained at 0.187 inch would have a coarser texture and greater density than grass maintained at 0.063 inch. Therefore, turf maintained at the lower mowing height would have fewer leaves to cut, and fewer leaves to be missed, during the initial cut. Thus, it seems reasonable that a lower green speed would result from double cutting greens that are maintained at ultralow mowing heights.

The data also verifies the management practices utilized by some golf course superintendents. I recall a tale of a superintendent who took over a course with bent/*Poa* greens that were maintained at a 0.115-inch mowing height. The new superintendent raised the mowing height to 0.141 inch but double cut three days a week to "get the speeds up" (Dennison, 2000). From what we know about mowing heights, diminishing returns, and double cutting, it is safe to assume that this turf manager met his objective.

Over the years, I have performed two long-term double cutting studies. The first study took place on a Pennlinks creeping bentgrass maintained at a mowing height of 0.156 inch. The study lasted ten weeks. The initial increase in green speed attributed to double cutting was approximately 3 inches. However, as the study progressed, the differences in green speed between single-mow and double-mow plots increased and the average difference was 6 inches.

In 2002 and 2003, I performed another double cutting study on a Providence creeping bentgrass green maintained at a 0.125-inch mowing height. During both seasons, the plots were double cut for three months. Once again, the original increase in green speed attributed to the first mowing was marginal (3 inches), but at the end of the first season, the average difference between single-mowed and doubled-mowed plots was 8 inches. After two full seasons of continued double mowing, nearly a foot increase (11 inches) in green speed was achieved at a mowing height of 0.125 inch.

The results from the double cutting studies are:

- At putting green mowing heights below 0.187 inch detectable increases in green speed should *not be expected* on the first day of double cutting. That is not to imply that you may not get an increase in speed of more than 6 inches the very first time you double cut— just don't bet on it.

- Double cutting daily at mowing heights as low as 0.125 inch will eventually result in detectable increases in green speed.

Combining these two points leads to the conclusion that when double cutting is practiced to increase green speeds for a club tournament, best results will be achieved if the double cutting is initiated several days prior to the event.

Given that many people, including myself, are not advocates of double cutting because of the perceived extra stress it puts on the turfgrass plant, I would be remiss if I did not mention something about turfgrass quality on the plots that we double cut for two straight years. Initially, the double-cut plots did not look very good, because they were scalped. However, the single-mow plots were also scalped (albeit minimally), most likely because the research was being performed on plots that had approximately an inch of thatch on them when the study was initiated. An aggressive cultural practice program was begun to decrease the amount of thatch on the plots. The cultural practices included core cultivation, using the Graden, and weekly to biweekly sand topdressing applications and verticutting. As we gained control of the thatch layer, the scalping subsided on the double-cut plots. As we went through the second year of the study, there were no apparent differences in turfgrass color or quality between the single-mow and double-mow plots.

Conclusions About Mowing and Green Speed

There are many potential problems associated with low mowing heights, so the overall goal of the golf course superintendent should be to find the highest possible mowing height at which his or her greens can be maintained with minimal complaints. A good place to start is to consider the point of diminishing returns in regard to mowing height and en-

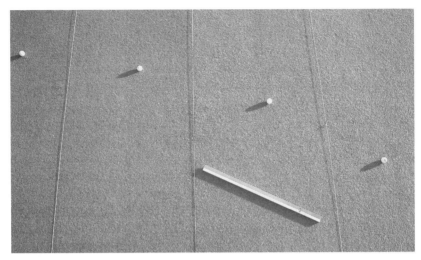

FIGURE 7-4. *From left to right, the mowing heights are 0.125, 0.157, 0.188, and 0.250 inches, the heights at which most greens have been mowed since 1930.*

courage your membership to find the ideal green speed on their course (Figure 7-4). Clearly, the golf course superintendent who determines the ideal green speed for his or her course is afforded the luxury of determining the highest possible height at which a green can be mowed and yet stay within the ideal green speed range.

Fertilization and Green Speed

*Fertilizers, fit only for agriculture, result in the sparse
velvety turf disappearing, being replaced by plantianes,
daises, and clover. And luscious grasses, which need an
enormous amount of mowing, weeding and upkeep.*
A. MACKENZIE, 1934

The Importance of Fertilizing

In an effort to maximize crop production, humankind began experimenting with the addition of fertilizer to the soil centuries ago. Today, following many years of trial and error and, in the past half century, advancements in technology and sound research, Western society has learned how to maximize its agricultural output to produce enough food to feed the world. Clearly, there are numerous advances that have allowed us to produce crops at these quantities, but without proper fertilization most of them would have had minimal impact.

We now understand that there are 16 essential elements (or nutrients) that plants need in order to grow, live, and/or function properly. Turfgrass is unique in agriculture as it is the only crop I know of in which we generally do *not* desire more growth. During establishment, the faster a grass germinates and fills in to the desired density, the better, but once that density has been achieved, most of us would prefer the grass to stop growing vertically so we do not have to mow it. It is this desire that has led to the widespread acceptance of plant growth regulators (PGRs) in the turfgrass industry.

Among the essential nutrients that turfgrass requires, nitrogen has been studied more than all others combined in terms of its impact on green speed. For this reason most of this chapter focuses on nitrogen, but it also discusses what is known about other nutrients and their effects on green speed.

Numerous publications list the considerations that go into preparing a fertilizing schedule, and most mention the word *budget*. Although budget may be considered a factor in regard to a particular product, it should not be a factor in determining the amount of a particular nutrient to be used in putting green maintenance. It is sometimes necessary to remind golfers that fertilizing turfgrass is not done merely for aesthetics but is an essential practice designed to satisfy the nutritional requirements of the plant so that it can survive and recuperate under daily traffic. Moreover, the owners of a golf course must be prepared to pay for the nutritional requirements of their greens.

On today's golf courses, the perfect putting green fertilizing schedule must take into consideration green speed, turfgrass color and quality, its recuperative potential, and its tolerance for a variety of stresses.

Nitrogen as a Fertilizer

It is common knowledge, and has also been well documented by research, that nitrogen enhances the aesthetic appeal of a turfgrass (makes it a darker green color), produces better growth, and increases its recuperative potential. For these reasons, nitrogen has long been the focal nutrient in the process of adjusting turfgrass fertility. No other nutrient is found in the plant tissue at higher quantities, and, in general, no other nutrient (with the possible exception of foliar iron) results in an undeniably better appearance.

In relation to the putting surface, the premise has clearly been that less growth allows greater green speed. The logical conclusion is that nitrogen rates should be minimized to maximize speed. This seems like a safe assumption, but perhaps we can benefit from the farmer's approach if we consider the law of diminishing returns in regard to nitrogen fertility.

For the farmer, the goal is to maximize productivity and quality with the least possible inputs. After all, this is the best way to maximize profit. Through a combination of sound record keeping and research, farmers can more readily pinpoint the proper amount of nitrogen to use to obtain the desired productivity. In terms of crop productivity (yield), "the addition of fertilizer causes increasing growth at a decreasing rate. Returns are diminishing. The first units of fertilizer produce a greater yield response than later units" (Foth and Ellis, 1988). In other words, at some point it is no longer productive for the farmer to add more nitrogen because yield will no longer increase.

For the golf course superintendent who is decreasing nitrogen rates to maximize green speed, it would seem intuitive that the reverse of the farmer's situation would hold true; that is, at some point, decreasing annual rates of nitrogen will no longer increase green speed but will result in decreases in the turfgrass color, quality, and recuperative potential. With that prospect in mind, it would be beneficial to identify the point (or highest nitrogen rate) at which speed would be maximized and benefits of nitrogen would be retained.

Recent History of Nitrogen Fertilization on Greens

Exactly how a putting green should be fertilized has been debated for years and many questions have yet to be answered, but because of concerns about green speed, I suspect we are probably getting closer to the solution, as illustrated in the following discussion.

In 1964, Michigan State University was teaching its turfgrass students that putting greens in Michigan should receive as much as 8.5 pounds of nitrogen per 1000 square feet annually. Nine years later, James Beard noted that, with creeping bentgrass, "nitrogen fertility requirement varies from 0.8 to 1.4 lb. per 1000 sq. ft. per growing month on greens" (Beard, 1973). Certainly, these pre-Stimpmeter nitrogen rates seem excessive, and in today's world, we would be justifiably concerned about groundwater contamination.

By the early 1980s, the pendulum swung excessively the other way, and some superintendents cut fertilizer back to "one pound of nitrogen per 1000 ft^2 per year" to attain maximum green speed on creeping bentgrass turf (Radko, 1985). Unfortunately, annual nitrogen applications as low as a pound per year resulted in turfgrass failure, as the soil's residual nitrogen was depleted after several years without any human input. The agronomic results of fertilizing with nitrogen at excessively low rates include thinner turf; increased moss, algae, and weeds; slower recuperation from ball marks, cups, aerification holes—and some superintendents losing their jobs (Figure 8-1). Certainly, this was not the intent of Eddie

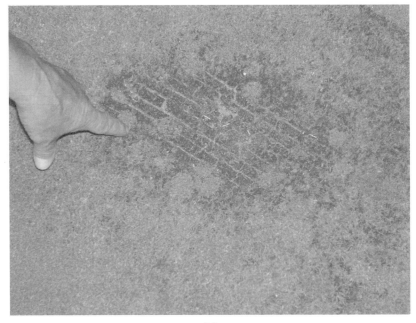

(a)

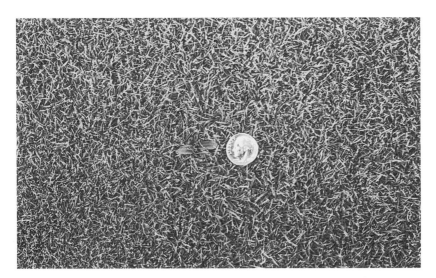

(b)

FIGURE 8-1 (*a,b*). *Excessively low mowing heights and N rates challenge the superintendent to control pests such as broadleaf weeds, moss, and algae. Both algae and broadleaf weeds are shown in Figure 8-1.*

Stimpson or the United States Golf Association (USGA) when they released the Stimpmeter.

Nitrogen and Green Speed

In terms of nitrogen fertilization and its relationship to green speed, five factors are worthy of consideration:

1. Annual nitrogen rate
2. Root zone mix and its potential impact on residual nitrogen
3. Frequency of fertilizer application
4. Fertilizer nitrogen carriers
5. Application technique (granular or liquid)

Annual Nitrogen Rate and the "4-inch Theory"

Clark Throssell performed a study of fertilizer rate in relation to green speed by applying nitrogen at the annual rates of 1, 2, 3, 4, and 6 pounds per 1000 square feet. He deduced from his research that the "relationship between nitrogen level and putting green speed is that for each pound of actual nitrogen applied per 1000 ft^2 during the season putting green speed will decrease approximately 4 inches" (Throssell, 1985). In the following discussion, Throssell's observation is referred to as the "4-inch theory"; that is, the 4-inch theory states that an annual decrease of nitrogen at the rate of 1 pound per 1000 square feet annually will result in a 4-inch increase in green speed.

It is important to note that Throssell also astutely added, "The relationship between nitrogen rate and speed may not fully portray the effect of nitrogen rate because of the wide variety of nitrogen sources used and the schedule of their application." However, it is advantageous to have a starting point, so the 4-inch theory will be considered as a general consensus in the following investigation of the research on nitrogen and green speed.

If the 4-inch theory held true, then in the decrease from Michigan State's 1964 recommendation of 8.5 pounds of nitrogen annually to the 1 pound of nitrogen applied annually by superintendents in the 1980s, green speed would have increased by 2 feet 10 inches because of nitrogen rate alone. Certainly this is a considerable change that even the novice

67

golfer would detect when putting, and, given the two extremes in annual nitrogen (N) rate, it also seems quite possible that a difference in
green speed of 2 feet 10 inches could be the result.

However, if the 4-inch theory really does hold true, then changing an
annual fertility program by 1.5 pounds of nitrogen per 1000 square feet
would *not* result in a perceivable impact on green speed, because it would
result in only a 6-inch difference. This suggests that all superintendents
who were fertilizing with 1 pound of nitrogen per 1000 square feet in
the mid-1980s could instead have been applying 2.5 pounds annually and
it would not have resulted in a noticeable change in the green speed on
their putting surfaces. In addition, their greens would have recuperated
better from the stresses of the game.

The 4-inch theory is intriguing in our quest for diminishing returns in
relationship to nitrogen, but how does it fit in with other nitrogen/green
speed studies? Certainly, there are many ways to fertilize putting greens.
Some superintendents use only granular fertilizers, others apply only liquids, and many use a combination of both. To further complicate the
equation, there are various types of root zones with different cation exchange capacities (CEC), which have an impact on the amounts of nutrients in the soil, and thus different pools of nutrients that may be more
readily available to the plants. In putting the 4-inch theory to the test, we
begin with the root zone.

Root Zone–Nitrogen Rate Interactions

As part of my dissertation at Michigan State University (MSU), I collected
Stimpmeter measurements on greens constructed with different root
zones, fertilized at different rates. The putting green root zone mixes included in the study were an 80:20 (sand: peat v/v) mixture constructed
to USGA recommendations; an 80:10:10 (sand: soil: peat v/v) mixture
built with subsurface tile drainage; and an undisturbed sandy clay loam
"push up" native soil. For each putting green root zone mixture there
were 3- by 17-foot plots that received 6 pounds of nitrogen annually (applied in 1-pound increments) and other 3- by 17-foot plots that received
3 pounds of nitrogen annually (applied in ½-pound increments). The first
and final applications of the year were urea (fast-release N), and the other
four applications were made with Nutralene (a methylene urea product
categorized as slow-to-intermediate in regard to nitrogen release from the
fertilizer granule). The study ran four full years.

In regard to the 4-inch theory, a 12-inch difference in green speed would be anticipated between the 6-pound and 3-pound annual rates. However, during the first year of the study, only one date resulted in statistically significant data between the lower rate of nitrogen and the higher rate. In that first year, the lower rate of nitrogen (3 pounds N per 1000 square feet) resulted in a green speed that averaged 3 inches faster than that produced with the higher rate of nitrogen (6 pounds, N per 1000 square feet).

During the second and third years of the study, every Stimpmeter measurement resulted in statistically faster green speeds on plots fertilized with the lower rate of nitrogen. In the second year of the study, the average difference in speed between the two rates of nitrogen was approximately 5 inches, and during the third year, the average difference in green speed was 7.5 inches (Table 8-1).

The implication is obvious: reducing the amount of nitrogen applied to a green does *not* necessarily result in an immediate increase in green speed that could be perceived by the average golfer. The question that needs to be considered is why did the difference in green speed exacerbate over time?

In most cases, finer-textured soils (clays) have higher cation exchange capacities (CEC) than coarser (sandy) soils, and more organic matter as well. In addition, the higher a soil's CEC and organic matter content, the greater its nutrient retention.

Given these facts of soil science, it may be anticipated that of the three root zones in the study (80:20, 80:10:10, and the sandy clay loam), the native soil green would have the highest CEC and therefore the greatest nutrient retention. Soil tests taken from 1997 to 2000 indicated that the native soil green had a significantly greater percentage of total nitrogen than the other two root zones during all four years. In addition, there were no significant differences in the amount of total nitrogen between

TABLE 8-1
Annual Nitrogen Rate

	1998	1999	2000
6 pounds N/year	9.70'	8.81'	8.66'
3 pounds N/year	9.96'	9.21'	9.29'
Average difference in green speed	3"	5"	7.5"

the 80:20 and the 80:10:10 root zones. In 1999 and 2000, the plots were sampled for inorganic forms of nitrogen, and once again the native soil green had significantly more ammonium (NH_4^+) below the topdressing layer than the other two root zones.

These retained nutrients should have been available for use by the plants during times when inputs (both natural and man-made) were low. If this were true, we would further expect that over a period of time without additional nitrogen inputs, the turfgrass plants would begin to utilize the residual nitrogen in the soil. In sandier soils, there would be less residual nitrogen to utilize as compared with the finer-textured soil.

During the first two years of the putting green root zone study with the two different nitrogen rates (6 and 3 pounds N per year), there were no interactions between green speed and nitrogen rate (meaning that the root zone soil type had no effect on the green speed differences that resulted from the different nitrogen rates). However, during the third year of the study, there were three interactions, between root zone and nitrogen rate, and for all three interactions, the native soil green (highest CEC and most residual nitrogen) produced the least noticeable difference in green speed between the two nitrogen rates (Table 8-2).

The data is interesting in that it verifies what several superintendents have told me about their experience of applying as little as 1 pound of nitrogen per year in the mid-1980s; that is, it appeared to them that things

TABLE 8-2

Differences in Green Speed Attributed to Two Annual Nitrogen Rates, as Applied on Penncross Creeping Bentgrass Plots with Three Different Root Zones, All Maintained at a 0.156-inch Mowing Height

| | Type of Root Zone | | |
	80:20	80:10:10	Sandy Clay Loam
6 pounds N/year	8.82 feet	9.02 feet	9.12 feet
3 pounds N/year	9.58 feet	9.78 feet	9.41 feet
Difference in green speed	9 inches	9 inches	3.5 inches
6 pounds N/year	8.69 feet	9.09 feet	8.99 feet
3 pounds N/year	9.45 feet	9.65 feet	9.41 feet
Difference in green speed	9 inches	7 inches	5 inches
6 pounds N/year	7.91 feet	7.81 feet	7.77 feet
3 pounds N/year	8.66 feet	8.63 feet	8.14 feet
Difference in green speed	9 inches	10 inches	4.5 inches

were going fine for the first year or two with the reduced rates, but in hindsight they determined that the residual nitrogen that had been built up in the root zone from previous years had finally diminished; the greens had become chlorotic and their recuperative ability decreased.

The data presented in Table 8-2 is also interesting because (1) at both nitrogen rates there is never a noticeable difference in green speed between any of the root zones and (2) after three years of fertilizing at the two different nitrogen rates, the sandier root zones were inching closer to the difference we would anticipate when considering the 4-inch theory.

Nitrogen Frequency and Its Effect on Green Speed

Whether for the sake of convenience, the need to control fertilizer placement, or because of the demands for faster green speeds, it is apparent that more superintendents are preferring liquid applications of nitrogen over the once-traditional granular applications. The terms *liquid* and *foliar*, referring to applications of fertilizer, are often used synonymously; however, there can be differences between the two methods that are worthy of comment.

Both types are applied as liquids, but *foliar application* implies that the nutrients are allowed to be absorbed through the leaf tissue. Liquid applications are not necessarily absorbed through the plant tissue, because they can be applied in a volume of water that results in most of the nutrients being washed off the leaf tissue during application, or the nutrient rate can be high enough that the manager purposely washes the nutrients off the plant tissue by applying irrigation immediately after the liquid application. The fertilizer is applied as a liquid, but is taken up via the roots like a traditional granular fertilizer.

In 1995, a study was designed to investigate the impact of various nitrogen carriers, applied at different frequencies, on green speed and turfgrass quality. In this study, a liquid fertilizer (Nutraculture 28-8-18) and two granular nitrogen products were applied at the rates of 0.25 and 0.16 pounds N per 1000 square feet every 7 days on a Penncross creeping bentgrass green. A final treatment of Nutralene (a slow-to-intermediate nitrogen-release product that is primarily methylene urea) was applied every 28 days at the rates of 1 and 0.64 pounds N per 1000 square feet. In short, all plots received either 1 pound or 0.64 pound of nitrogen over the 28-day period, with the products applied at different frequencies.

The hypothesis was that applying nitrogen at light frequent intervals (every 7 days) would result in enhanced turfgrass quality and faster green speeds as compared with applying equivalent rates at monthly (every 28 days) intervals. The study included Penncross creeping bentgrass plots that were maintained at a $\frac{3}{16}$-inch mowing height. The study ran from mid-May to September, with Stimpmeter measurements generally taken every 7 days (prior to the weekly application of fertilizers).

Of the 10 Stimpmeter measurements recorded, few resulted in statistically significant differences. In a nutshell, there were no meaningful differences (none greater than 6 inches) in green speed associated with the frequency of the fertilizer applications or the nitrogen carrier.

In addition, annual nitrogen rates on the plots totaled either 4 or 2.56 pounds per 1000 square feet. Given the 4-inch theory, we would expect a difference in green speed of no more than 6 inches. The average difference between the two rates was that plots receiving 2.56 pounds N per year averaged 2 inches faster green speeds than plots that received 4 pounds N per year.

I was quite surprised by the results of the study. I had expected that the liquid application at the frequency of every seven days would result in faster green speeds than monthly granular applications of slower-nitrogen-release carriers.

Fast-Release versus Slow-Release Nitrogen Carriers

Partly because of the results of the aforementioned study and partly because superintendents were once again using the 1-pound annual rate of nitrogen, a study was initiated in the spring of 2000 to investigate the impact of various methods of "spoon-feeding" nitrogen on turfgrass quality and green speed, as compared with monthly applications of granular nitrogen with different release rates. In this study, urea (46-0-0) and methylene urea (40-0-0) were applied monthly (every 30 days) at the rate of 1 pound N per 1000 square feet, resulting in an annual rate of 4 pounds N per 1000 square feet.

Also included in the study were a total of four different spoon-feeding programs, which are discussed later in this chapter. For reasons of clarity, a complete listing of all treatments included in the study appears in Table 8-3. The Stimpmeter data is presented in a series of figures that make the most useful product (treatment) comparisons.

In all of the related figures that follow, the y-axis is Stimpmeter measurements reported in feet; they are presented in 6-inch increments be-

TABLE 8-3

Treatments Used in a 2000 Michigan State University Fertilizer Green Speed Study Designed to Evaluate the Impact of Different Nitrogen Carriers, Different Nitrogen Rates, and Different Nitrogen Programs on Green Speed and Turfgrass Quality

	Treatment Number and Products Used in the Treatment	Application Method	Product Rate/1000 square feet per Application	Application Interval	Annual N Rate/1000 Square Feet
1	M-urea 40-0-0	Granular	1.0 pound N	30 days	4 pounds
2	Urea 46-0-0	Granular	1.0 pound N	30 days	4 pounds
3	Starter fertilizer 14-28-10	Granular	1.0 pound N	April 28[a]	2.1 pounds
	Foliar fertilizer 28-7-14	Foliar	0.1 pound N	10 days	
4	Natural organic 6-2-0	Granular	1.0 pound N	April 28[a]	2.1 pounds
	Foliar fertilizer 28-7-14	Foliar	0.1 pound N	10 days	
5	Foliar fertilizer 28-7-14	Foliar	0.1 pound N	10 days	1.2 pounds
6	Check plot (no fertility)	—	—	—	—
7	Foliar fertilizer 28-7-14 tank-mixed with Primo Maxx 1EC	Foliar	0.1 pound N	10 days	1.2 pound
		Foliar	0.04 fluid ounces	10 days	
8	M-urea 40-0-0 and	Granular	1.0 pound N	30 days	4 pounds
	Primo Maxx 1EC	Foliar	0.125 fluid ounces	30 days	

[a]Granular applications in treatments 3 and 4 were made one time for the season.

73

cause any measurement within that increment would not be noticeable to the average golfer.

During the months of June, July, and August, Stimpmeter measurements were taken on the plots at five-day intervals, thus totaling six green speed measurements per treatment per month. When Stimpmeter measurements were taken on days that fertilizer treatments were applied, the measurements were always taken prior to treatment application.

It would be logical to anticipate that different granular nitrogen carriers would result in differences in green speed because they have different nitrogen release rates. Included in Figure 8-2 is an unfertilized check plot along with green speed measurements comparing methylene urea (M-urea) to urea (a 100 percent water-soluble-nitrogen (WSN) fast-release nitrogen source).

The nonfertilized check plot green speed measurements are included in the figure to illustrate the significant impact that environmental factors can have on green speed. The dips in the check plots' green speed are synchronous with rainfall events, with the largest dip coinciding with a thunderstorm. Also, as expected, the nonfertilized plot generally produced the greatest green speed.

In regard to the two granular nitrogen treatments, of the 18 dates when Stimpmeter measurements were taken, only one resulted in a difference

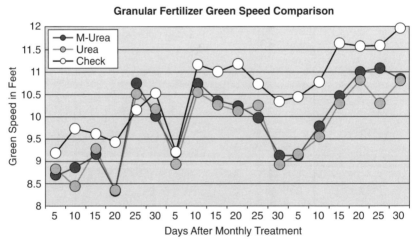

FIGURE 8-2. *When applied at identical rates and frequencies, research indicates there are no meaningful differences in green speed between fast and intermediate nitrogen-release fertilizers.*

that was greater than 6 inches. Prior to the study, I had anticipated that use of the urea would have resulted in slower green speeds for the first two weeks following the application (because it is a faster nitrogen-release product), with the methylene urea being slower during the final two weeks of the month (since it is a slower-release product). From these results it can be theorized that at monthly fertilization rates as high as 1 pound of nitrogen during the growing season, there should be no difference in green speed attributable to different nitrogen carriers.

Monthly Applications of Nitrogen and Plant Growth Regulators

Numerous studies have been designed to examine the impact of plant growth regulators on green speed. This subject is discussed further in Chapter 10, but at this point we consider the difference in green speed produced by methylene urea applied at 1 pound of nitrogen every 30 days, with and without Primo Maxx applied immediately afterward at the labeled rate of 0.125 fluid ounces.

Stimpmeter measurements (Figure 8-3) obtained from the study showed that the Primo Maxx treatment produced meaningful increases in green speed on 5 of the 18 dates on which green speed measurements

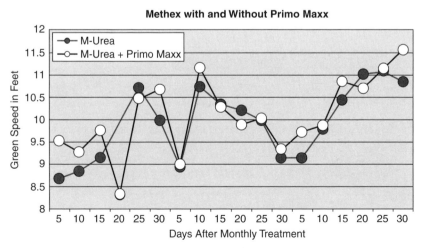

FIGURE 8-3. *While PGRs have many benefits for the putting surface, research indicates enhanced green speed is not one of them.*

were obtained. There were no meaningful trends in the data, although 20 days after treatment the greens treated with the Primo Maxx tended to have significant decreases in speed. The average annual difference in green speed was that the plots treated with Primo were 3 inches faster than plots not treated with Primo.

A Comparison of Liquid Nitrogen Programs

It has been suggested that nitrogen is absorbed much more quickly than phosphorous through the turfgrass leaf tissue (Beard 1973). If this were true, then superintendents who consistently foliar fed would eventually observe symptoms of phosphorous deficiency on their turfgrass (especially in a sandy root zone). Although I am unable to offer documentation, I have observed the spindly growth and purplish hue attributed to phosphorus deficiency on greens that have been on a strict foliar feeding management program (Figure 8-4).

There are many organisms in the soil that benefit from fertilizer application techniques that feed the soil. In turn, some of these microor-

FIGURE 8-4. *Sand greens that are on a strict program of foliar feeding sometimes display the purplish discoloration of a phosphorous deficiency, as evident in these research plots.*

ganisms benefit the turfgrass plant. So, although I am a staunch advocate of foliar feeding turfgrass, I also think it is prudent to feed the soil at least once a year.

It was this thought process that led to the formulation of the four different foliar nitrogen programs included in this green speed study. All four foliar treatments received 28-7-14 applied in solution every ten days at the rate of 0.10 pounds of nitrogen per 1000 square feet, resulting in a monthly foliar rate of 0.30 pound N and an annual foliar applied rate of 1.20 pounds N per 1000 square feet.

One of the foliar treatments was simply as stated earlier; two others were initiated with 1 pound of nitrogen applied as a granular product with either a starter fertilizer or Milorganite, and the final "spoon-feeding" treatment was tank mixed with Primo Maxx 1 EC at one-third the labeled rate.

The 18 green speed measurements obtained from the plots are presented in Figure 8-5. Scrutiny of the data makes it abundantly clear that there were no significant differences in green speed that resulted from any of the treatments included in the study.

In terms of a seasonal average, the 0.10 pound N, both with and without Primo Maxx, resulted in an average annual green speed of approxi-

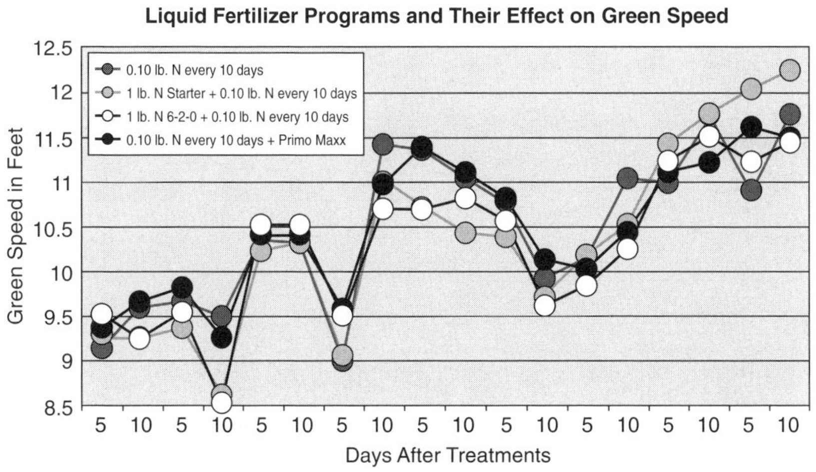

Liquid Fertilizer Programs and Their Effect on Green Speed

FIGURE 8-5. *Tank mixing Primo Maxx with a spoon-feeding nitrogen program and adding 1 pound of nitrogen per 1000 sq. ft. as a granular had no impact on green speed when compared to a spoon-feeding-only program.*

mately 10 feet 6 inches. The treatments that were initiated with 1 pound N in a granular form (to feed the soil) resulted in the slowest green speed, but they averaged only 2 inches slower than the fastest plots.

Of course, we would be negligent if we did not consider turfgrass quality with these different programs. In Figure 8-6 are turfgrass quality ratings that were obtained over the duration of the study. Turfgrass quality is generally rated on a scale of 1 to 9, where 1 = dead or chlorotic turfgrass, 9 = excellent putting green turfgrass quality, and ratings of 5.5 and above are considered acceptable.

As in most fertilization studies, the nonfertilized treatment always results in the lowest quality rating. The foliar only treatment received an acceptable rating on only three of ten days that ratings were taken. However, the 0.10-pound N treatments that originated with a granular soil feeding of starter fertilizer or a natural organic fertilizer achieved ac-

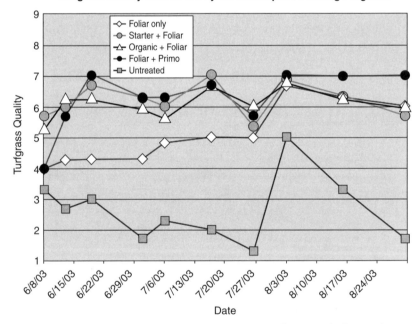

FIGURE 8-6. *While the Primo Maxx or the addition of 1 pound of granular nitrogen per 1000 sq. ft. had no effect on green speed compared to a spoon-feeding-only program, they clearly resulted in far better turfgrass quality.*

ceptable ratings most of the time. In addition, the foliar treatment tank mixed with the one-third labeled rate Primo Maxx also achieved an acceptable quality rating most of the time.

As stated earlier in this book, I do not believe that speed kills. What the superintendent needs to do is to make the best agronomically sound decisions to get the speed desired. Considering that plots receiving the additional 1 pound of nitrogen earlier in the year showed no perceptible reduction in green speed and the turfgrass quality was far superior to that of plots receiving foliar feeding alone, it seems agronomically responsible to make certain to add a pound of nitrogen (and other nutrients) in a granular form at some point during the season.

Furthermore, many superintendents are under the assumption that plant growth regulators (PGRs) increase green speed. Yet, the data is fairly consistent in showing that PGRs do *not* increase green speed in a predictable manner that would allow them to be part of a calculated management scheme. However, PGRs, such as the Primo Maxx in this study, can enhance turfgrass color and quality and allow the turf manager to get adequate lateral growth with lower rates of nitrogen.

The results of this study leave me wishing that we had included a treatment that originated with 1 pound of a granular treatment, followed by 0.10 pound of nitrogen, tank mixed with one-third labeled rate Primo Maxx every ten days. My assumption is that this treatment would have resulted in even better turfgrass quality, with no perceptible difference in green speed, than the foliar only treatment.

Monthly Applications versus Granular Spoon-Feeding

As previously observed, applications of liquid and granular fertilizer at identical rates of nitrogen resulted in no meaningful difference in green speed. However, because many superintendents have decreased their rates and changed application techniques in an effort to increase green speed, it is important to consider the differences in green speed resulting from monthly granular applications of 1 pound N and those achieved by spoon-fed liquid applications at the rate of 0.10 pound N every ten days.

As expected, the data presented in Figure 8-7 indicates that the foliar application of 0.10 pound N every 10 days resulted in noticeably faster green speeds as compared with the 1-pound N monthly treatment. The

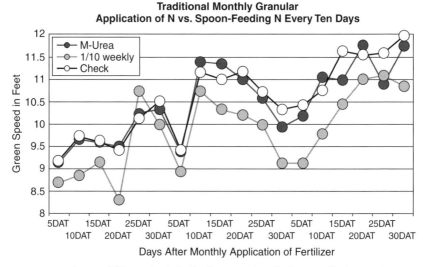

FIGURE 8-7. *As would be expected, the lower rate of nitrogen that was spoon-fed resulted in a faster green speed than the higher monthly application of nitrogen.*

annual average showed that the speed achieved with 0.10 pound N every 10 days was 8 inches faster than that procured with 1 pound N every 30 days. The difference between the two treatments was 2.8 pounds N per 1000 square feet per year, which means we could have anticipated a difference of approximately 11 inches with respect to the 4-inch theory. Interestingly, there was only a 1.5-inch difference in green speed between the foliar treatment and the nonfertilized treatment.

Ultralow Nitrogen Rates to Enhance Green Speed

Like slight decreases in mowing height, slight decreases in nitrogen rate do not result in noticeable increases in green speed. In an effort to illustrate the significance, or lack thereof, of the impact ultralow spoon-feeding rates have on green speed, a study was initiated at Michigan State University in the spring of 2003.

In this study, Emerald Isle NutriRational foliar fertilizer was applied at the rates of 0.04, 0.06, 0.08, and 0.12 pound N per 1000 square feet every 14 days on an A4 creeping bentgrass green that was walk-mowed at ⅛-inch mowing height six days a week.

Green speed was measured on 38 dates during the spring and summer of 2003, resulting in significant differences on only two occasions. That statistically significant differences in green speed did not result from the rates of nitrogen used in the study clearly indicates that there is no immediate green speed response to decreasing already low spoon-fed nitrogen rates.

It must be noted that turfgrass quality ratings were taken 13 times during the study. On every occasion, the data was statistically significant, and on every date, the higher rate of nitrogen resulted in a rating of significantly greater quality.

Conclusions About Nitrogen and Green Speed

Given the various nitrogen carriers and formulations, the potential rates and application techniques, the numerous putting green root zone mixes, and the ever-increasing numbers of turfgrass cultivars that can be used on a putting surface, there is an infinite amount of research that could be done regarding nitrogen and green speed. Furthermore, if anyone is contemplating an effort to address this need, it would be most helpful if such a study on nitrogen and green speed ran for several years to further investigate the long-term effects on the plant, as well as the speed. However, from the data that has been generated to date, we can make some pertinent conclusions that should be helpful in regard to nitrogen, green speed, and turfgrass agronomy.

From Clark Throssel's early work with nitrogen rates, we formulated the 4-inch theory as a benchmark for annual nitrogen rates. (The 4-inch theory states that for every annual change of 1 pound N per 1000 square feet, we should expect a difference in green speed of 4 inches.)

Comparing the 4-inch theory with the results of all other data regarding different nitrogen rates, the difference in green speed attributed to the different rates was always within the 4-inch expectation. Considering the longest-running study that compared 3 pounds N per 1000 square feet annually with 6 pounds N per 1000 square feet annually, the largest annual difference was approximately 9 inches after three years of applying nitrogen at these differing rates on predominantly sandy root zones. This suggests that the 4-inch theory provides a safe rule of thumb for managing green speed, because it implies that raising an annual nitrogen rate as much as 1.5 pounds N per 1000 square feet will *not* result in a noticeable difference in green speed, yet the turf color and recuperative potential will be increased.

Other pertinent conclusions regarding nitrogen and the green speed data include the following:

- Reductions in nitrogen rates should not be expected to result in an immediately noticeable increase in green speed, which is due in part to residual nitrogen that is most likely present in the root zone.

- Comparisons of identical rates of nitrogen with different nitrogen carriers having different release rates resulted in no noticeable differences in green speed.

- When annual nitrogen rates were identical but were delivered at different frequencies, there was *not* a noticeable change in green speed.

- Weekly liquid applications that result in the same nitrogen rate as monthly granular applications did *not* result in any noticeable change in green speed.

- An application of a granular nitrogen fertilizer at the rate of 1 pound N per 1000 square feet to feed the soil (and possibly supply other important nutrients to the plant) resulted in *no* noticeable difference in green speed on plots that received a liquid application at a rate of 0.10 pound N per 1000 square feet every 10 days. Moreover, plots receiving the additional granular fertilizer had far superior turfgrass quality.

- Tank mixing Primo Maxx 1 EC at one-third the labeled rate with a fertilizer rate of 0.10 pound N per 1000 square feet every 10 days resulted in far superior turfgrass quality, as compared with plots that received the identical nitrogen treatment without the PGR.

- There were *no* differences in green speed attributed to foliar treatments of fertilizer applied every 14 days at the rates of 0.04, 0.06, 0.08, and 0.12 pound N per 1000 square feet.

Considering the importance of nitrogen to the health, density, recuperative potential, and aesthetic appearance of the putting surface, it would be negligent to withhold this nutrient more than necessary to increase green speed.

Potassium Fertilization on the Golf Course

Potassium is an essential element that plants need to survive; however, in terms of turfgrass fertilization, there remain legitimate questions regarding annual potassium rates.

As discussed previously, nitrogen fertilization rates and the frequency of applications have changed dramatically over the years. In regard to fertilizing turfgrass with potassium, it is not so much a question of the rates as whether to fertilize with potassium at all and the ratio of nitrogen to potassium. In 1912, A. D. Hall wrote, "No fertilizer containing potash should ever be used on golf course putting greens" (Isaac and Canaway, 1987). This adamant view on the use of potassium on greens was mellowed a bit in 1925, as Charles Oakley suggested the possibility of using potassium, but stated that where there was a sufficiency of potassium, none should be supplied. However, I am not certain what a "sufficiency" of potassium was at that time.

In 1979, research performed by Nick Christians and colleagues led them to conclude that potassium may play a more important role in turfgrass fertilization than had previously been realized. In their greenhouse experiment, they noticed that as the level of potassium increased, less nitrogen was required to attain maximum turfgrass quality, and concluded that additional work under field conditions was required to evaluate the importance of the relationship between nitrogen and potassium rates (Christians et al., 1979).

Since Christians's greenhouse experiment, numerous studies have been performed to study the effects of potassium on the turfgrass plant, but there is still no consensus among turfgrass managers as to the proper potassium fertilization rates (Sartain, 2002). Furthermore, no one has yet determined with any precision what levels of phosphorus and potassium in soils are optimum for turfgrass growth (Turgeon, 1991). Many turfgrass managers believe increasing potassium rates relative to those of nitrogen will lead to improved disease resistance; heat, drought, and wear tolerance; enhanced root growth; and ultimately, increased green speed due to increased turgor pressure and enhancement of upright growth.

An analysis of commercial fertilizers for turfgrass reflects the change in the philosophy of turfgrass managers regarding potassium fertilization. Twenty years ago a common analysis was 23-3-3, but today analysis such as 20-3-15 and 30-0-30 are common as turf managers are applying high levels of potassium and very low levels of nitrogen (Christians, 1998).

Potassium and Green Speed

It may be logical to assume that increasing potassium rates will increase green speed by increasing the plant's turgor pressure and enhancing its upright growth. It is this assumption that has led many a golf course superintendent (including me) to apply potassium to the putting surface a week or two before a club championship or any another important tournament.

The question is, "Is there any data to validate this assumption?" In 1988–89, Nus and Haupt performed a potassium rate study on a 4-year-old stand of Penncross creeping bentgrass. They applied potassium at the rates of 0, 2, 4, 6, and 8 pounds of potassium per year. From the data made available, they measured green speed on two occasions, and on both occasions, no meaningful differences in green speed were obtained. Of course, there were only two measurements, and, as they pointed out in their paper, it is important to take into consideration soil test information (Nus and Haupt, 1989).

From 1997 to 2000, I performed a study on three different putting green root zone mixes that were fertilized with different annual rates of potassium. The putting green root zone mixes included in the study were an 80:20 (sand: peat v/v) mixture constructed to United States Golf Association (USGA) specifications; an 80:10:10 (sand: soil: peat v/v) mixture built 12 inches deep with subsurface tile drainage; and an undisturbed sand clay loam (58 percent sand, 21 percent silt, and 21 percent clay) native soil. The plots were previously established with Penncross creeping bentgrass that was mowed six days per week at a 0.156-inch mowing height. Potassium rates included in the study were 0, 4, and 8 pounds of (K_2O) per 1000 square feet annually.

From June 1997 to August 2000, 17 green speed measurements were obtained from the research green (Figure 8-8). The second-to-last measurement obtained was the only measurement that resulted in statistically significant data, and on that one occasion, the check plot (that is, the plots that received no potassium) produced the fastest green speed. However, though the data was statistically significant, there was less than a 3-inch difference between the 0 pound and the 4 and 8 pound annual rates.

Green Speed Measurements Obtained from Plots Fertilized with Three Different Potassium Rates from 1998–2000.

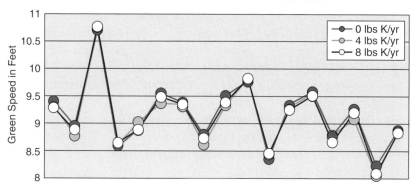

FIGURE 8-8. *On research plots, different potassium rates have resulted in no meaningful differences in green speed.*

The conclusion was that potassium rate had *no* effect on green speed, regardless of the putting green root zone mix.

One of the most interesting aspects of the data presented in Figure 8-8 is the tight grouping of the data. Some believe that the Stimpmeter is not a very accurate tool. Scientists, as well as golf course superintendents, who have used the Stimpmeter often rationalize hard-to-explain measurements as the natural variability that exists with the instrument. Data from the potassium rates in this study refute the notion the Stimpmeter is not an accurate device, as the range of green speed measurements from the treatments were less than ½ inch to 2.4 inches, with an average magnitude of approximately 1 inch. This data set suggests that the Stimpmeter is a more precise tool than some believe and support the conclusion of Joe Duich (1983), that with a limited amount of experience, an operator can use the Stimpmeter with a high degree of precision.

Of course, as Nus and Haupt pointed out, it is important to consider soil test information when performing potassium research to determine whether root zones are deficient in potassium. Therefore, during the study, soil samples were collected annually from 1998 to 2000. In regard to the different putting green root zones, the 80:20 mix averaged 52 pounds K/A and the native soil green averaged 284 pounds K/A (potassium per acre). According to recommendations for potash, the 80:20 root zone should receive 5 pounds K_2O/1000 square feet annually and the native root zone should receive 1.5 pounds K_2O per 1000 square feet annually, based on MSU soil test recommendations.

In short, there clearly was a difference in the amount of K_2O in the different putting green root zones, as well as on plots treated with the different potassium rates, over the four-year period. However, even though the K_2O levels were different and considered to be deficient, there were no corresponding differences in green speed attributed to the differences in the soil test results.

Given the data that exists regarding green speed and potassium, it may seem logical to conclude that potassium has no meaningful effect on green speed. However, that may be an oversimplification, as there are two points worthy of consideration.

First, research performed by Dest and Guillard (2001) suggests that the release of potassium from primary minerals in some root zones with high sand content proceeds at rates to satisfy bentgrass requirements for potassium. In other words, even though soil test results indicate that potassium is deficient, in many sandy soils it is still being released naturally from the sand at rates to satisfy the potash requirements of bentgrasses. If this is true, then any greens of bentgrass growing in this type of sand may never truly have a potassium deficiency. This also suggests that in my study, even though the soil test results indicated deficiencies in potash in the sandier root zones, perhaps there really was no deficiency within the plant; the primary minerals in the root zones may have been releasing potassium fast enough to satisfy the bentgrass.

In addition, there is clearly more data in the literature that indicates the benefits of potassium fertilization on Bermudagrass as compared with bentgrass. Unfortunately, none that I have been able to uncover investigate the impact of potassium rates on the green speed of this warm-season grass.

In conclusion, no data has ever been reported indicating that potassium has any effect on green speed, even though soil test results have indicated deficiencies in the macronutrient.

Phosphorous

A quick search of the literature indicates there has been only one study reporting green speed measurements as they relate to differences in phosphorous fertilization. In the study, the rates reported were 0 and 50 kg ha^{-1} yr^{-1} P, or 0 pounds and 1 pound P per 1000 square feet per year. In the research, the aforementioned phosphorus rates were applied on plots receiving five different annual nitrogen rates, ranging from 0.7 to 13 pounds N per 1000 square feet per year. Results from the study seem to indicate that at nitrogen rates at or below 4.8 pounds N per year, the difference in the phosphorus rates resulted in no meaningful difference in green speed. Furthermore, at nitrogen rates ranging from approximately 8 to 13 pounds per 1000 square feet per year, the higher phosphorus rate resulted in a decrease in green speed. Exactly how much of a decrease in speed occurred is impossible to interpret, since the "ball roll" measurements were obtained with a homemade version of a Stimpmeter (thus the numbers are not transferable).

This is hardly conclusive evidence, but it is all I have been able to uncover in the literature at this time. Yet it seems clear that judicious applications of phosphorus and nitrogen at moderate rates are good for the turf and the environment and are not detrimental to green speed.

Micronutrients

There are many micronutrient concoctions on the market promised to enhance green speed. Although I am not implying that these products do not work, there is a complete lack of evidence in the literature that micronutrients improve green speed. Yet, there is still some valuable information to be considered.

In 1992, Agnew and Schmidt reported on a micronutrient study they performed on a Penncross creeping bentgrass research green at the Iowa State University Horticulture Research Station. Treatments included Agri-Plex For-X, Agri-Plex Fe 8%, Agri-Plex Fe 8% Mn 2%, Sprint 138 Fe, Sprint 330 Fe, FeSO$_3$ Mn SO$_3$, and a control plot. Ten Stimpmeter measurements were made on the plots from May through September, and fewer than half resulted in statistically significant differences. In short, these micronutrient sources had a minimal positive or negative effect on green speed.

Micronutrients are often applied to enhance color and/or to help alleviate deficiencies attributed to the high pH levels often found in sand-based greens. Most of us have observed the benefits of enhanced color with an iron application. Moreover, essential elements are, in fact, essential; that is, they provide a function that no other nutrient can perform within the plant, and therefore a lack of such nutrients can lead to plant death. Given this premise, as turf managers we must accept the fact that having adequate levels of micronutrients (such as iron and manganese) may enhance the plant's tolerance of drought, cold, heat, disease, and traffic.

It is imperative that the turfgrass plant receives the proper nutrition. Given the data from Agnew and Schmidt, the positive side of the story is that adding these micronutrient packages did not decrease green speed, which implies that proper nutrition with micronutrients can be attempted with confidence that there will be no long-term loss of green speed.

Conclusions Regarding Fertilization and Green Speed

Clearly, there are many "holes" in the data regarding particular nutrients and their effects on green speed. It is not my intent to ignore the needs of the superintendent with warm-season grasses; unfortunately, all the research on nutrients that I have been able to uncover has been done on cool-season grasses. The studies referenced in this chapter are those that I believe give the clearest answers to questions regarding nutrients and their impact on green speed. Along with some conclusions drawn from these studies, however, I present further references and data so that the reader can draw his or her own conclusions.

With the exception of nitrogen, it is safe to assume that the use of essential elements will not result in decreasing green speed unless those elements are lacking in the plant. If a nutrient is truly deficient in the plant, we can assume that the plant is growing at a less than optimum rate. The addition of the lacking nutrient *might* enhance growth, which in turn *might* decrease green speed. In any case, proper nutrition must be maintained for the health of the plant and the game of golf. In the case of potassium, if it is truly limited in the plant, there is a possibility that the addition of this nutrient may enhance green speed; the dilemma at this time seems to be determining whether the plant is truly deficient in this nutrient. On the positive side, excessive rates of potassium did not decrease green speed.

It appears that the benefits of using at least one granular fertilizer application a year to feed the soil and the numerous beneficial microorganisms, to keep the turfgrass plant healthy, outweigh the minimal negative impact (far less than a 6-inch difference) of such a fertilization practice. The data also suggests that the 4-inch theory, in terms of nitrogen fertilization, is a good rule of thumb, as all data suggests that increasing annual nitrogen rates of as much as a pound a year will not have a noticeable impact on green speed.

The data further suggests that we can fertilize to enhance the speed of the greens and the health of the turf at the same time. Just as the greyhound and the racehorse are fed a proper diet not only to stay slim, but also to be strong enough to win the race, our greens must be fed not only for speed, but for their strength and recuperative potential as well.

From a historical perspective, since the release of the Stimpmeter superintendents have reduced nitrogen inputs. Although at certain times and at particular sites the nutritional reductions have been too severe, it is my belief that the Stimpmeter has guided us to more judicious fertilization rates. Throughout the history of our culture, we have fallen prey to the credo that more is better, but that is not always the case (recall King Midas and his quest for gold). Thus, it is hard for me to believe that 8 pounds N per 1000 square feet on bentgrass putting greens in Michigan is better than half that annual rate, which is now customarily applied. The Stimpmeter may actually have had a positive effect on the environment.

9

Lightweight Rolling: A Most Vexing Practice for Many Superintendents

Frequent rolling with light rollers, 3 foot or so in width, and weighing a hundredweight to a hundredweight and a half is undoubtedly beneficial, but the excessive use of the heavy roller used to be one of the commonest faults in greenkeeping.

COLT, 1906

History of Rolling

The game of golf thrived in England centuries before the manufacture of a mechanical mower, and for years I thought that rolling the putting surface took place more often than mowing. Unfortunately, I have never come across any document supporting such a conclusion. Yet, it certainly seems clear that the practice of rolling has existed as long as mowing and, moreover, that it has been controversial as long as it has been employed.

In 1901, greenkeeper Walter Davis wrote, "From May until October each green should be rolled daily with a light roller, rather than once or twice a week with a heavy one" (Travis, 1901). Davis's comment addressing roller weight and frequency reflect concerns that remain to this day. However, it was not until 1906 that Hutchinson defined light rollers as "3 foot or so in width, and weighing a hundredweight to a hundredweight and a half" (Hutchinson, 1906). A "hundredweight" in England is defined as 112 pounds; thus, according to Hutchinson, a lightweight roller would be defined as weighing between 112 and 168 pounds (see Figure 9-1).

Golf course research pioneers Piper and Oakley introduced the consideration of root zones into the roller equation, as they noted in 1921, "Excess rolling on sandy or sandy loam soils is practically impossible" (Piper and Oakley, 1921). For the next quarter century, numerous publications addressed roller frequency, weight, compaction, and soil texture without coming to any clear conclusions. Consequently, the practice of frequent rolling ceased at about this time, as turfgrass research showed a link between high levels of soil compaction and lack of turf root growth (DiPaola and Hartwiger, 1994), even though there was never any data concluding that rolling increased soil compaction.

Because of the demand for fast green speeds, the practice of lightweight rolling made a comeback in the mid-1980s. After all, if there was one thing most everyone agreed on with regard to rolling, it was that rolling significantly increased green speed. However, concerns that existed in the 1920s have remained, in that some golf course superintendents view rolling as a means of improving putting quality, while others

FIGURE 9-1. *Though these rollers are currently used on today's more manicured greens, they still fit Horace Hutchinson's 1906 definition of a light roller.*

believe rolling causes additional stress that makes management of putting greens more difficult (Hartwiger, 1996). Besides these near century-old concerns regarding compaction, there are additional concerns about aboveground turfgrass problems associated with continual season-long turf rolling and the possibility that pathogens may invade crushed tissues, resulting in diseased turf (Beard, 1994).

In the mid-1980s, if a golf course superintendent searched the literature for answers regarding the frequency, benefits, detriments, and recommended weight for green rollers, he or she would have found little research on rollers and the putting surface. One of the oldest practices in the game of golf had never been adequately researched. Did this "hole" in the research exist because the practice had fallen from grace for several decades, or because we thought we knew the answers, or perhaps a bit of both? Whatever the cause of the negligence, a few researchers began investigating the practice in the late 1980s, and now a great deal is known about rolling.

In Search of a Safe Frequency for Lightweight Rolling

How often, or at what frequency, can greens be rolled without detriment to the putting green turfgrass or the underlying root zone? Many superintendents continue to be apprehensive about rolling because they have been unable to answer this question.

Fortunately, since the early 1990s, several studies have considered the effects of season-long lightweight green rolling on soil compaction. By examining the methods and results of each of these studies, we can estimate the best rolling frequency for a putting surface.

Under the direction of George Hamilton, Pennsylvania State University (PSU) researchers collected data on the physical properties of the soil after rolling bentgrass plots grown on United States Golf Association (USGA)-recommended sand and native soil root zones. In this study, plots were rolled once or twice per week. The study ran two years, resulting in no differences in turfgrass quality, soil bulk density, or water infiltration on rolled plots as compared with nonrolled plots (Hamilton et al, 1994).

From 1995 to 2000, a lightweight rolling study was performed at Michigan State University (MSU) on three different putting green root zone mixes. Included in the study were 80:20 (sand: peat), 80:10:10 (sand: soil:

peat), and native (push-up) sandy clay loam root zone mixes, all seeded with Penncross creeping bentgrass in 1992. Rolling treatments included no rolling and rolling three times a week with an Olathe sidewinder roller (Figure 9-2). During all six years, data on the soils' physical properties was obtained from all three root zones that were rolled and not rolled. On every occasion, rolling resulted in no significant change in bulk density (soil compaction) or water infiltration, as compared with these conditions on the unrolled putting green plots.

There are two important facts that need to be considered in regard to the results of the MSU study: (1) The Olathe roller has three rollers, and the unit weight approximately 950 pounds without an operator. By current standards, the Olathe (which is no longer manufactured) is an extremely *heavy* lightweight roller, and (2) *all three* rootzones were on a light-frequent sand topdressing program, receiving sand every two to three weeks during the growing season, depending upon growing conditions. Without the addition of this sand, it is impossible to predict whether the rolling frequency of three times per week would have resulted in any negative effects on the turfgrass plant or root zone. Therefore, considering the longevity of the study and its results, a rolling

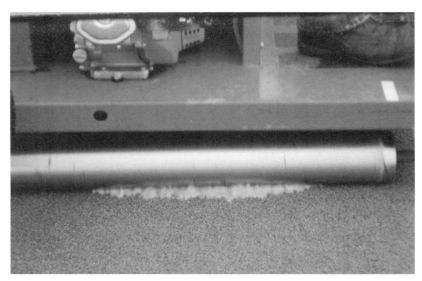

FIGURE 9-2. *Research plots in the Michigan State University rolling study were rolled three days a week, come rain or shine.*

frequency of three times per week on bentgrass greens on a frequent sand topdressing program should result in no detrimental effects to the soil or the turfgrass quality attributed solely to rolling.

When USGA agronomist Chris Hartwiger was at North Carolina State University (NCSU), he furthered our knowledge as he rolled bentgrass greens at the frequencies of zero, one, four, and seven times per week. As in the PSU study, plots rolled one time per week resulted in no reduction in turfgrass quality. However, rolling at the frequencies of four and seven times per week resulted in diminished turfgrass quality on plots growing in USGA-recommended sand root zones and plots having native soil root zones. Furthermore, during the first year of the two-year study, compaction increased on the native soil greens rolled four and seven times per week (DiPaola and Hartwiger, 1994). Considering that some superintendents roll daily for one or two weeks during and in preparation of a tournament, it is noteworthy that the diminished turfgrass quality attributed to lightweight rolling four and seven times per week was not immediate. The reduction in turfgrass quality at those frequencies took three to four weeks to become apparent.

Given the rolling frequencies and the results of the studies performed at PSU, MSU, and NCSU, three times per week, in a season-long lightweight rolling program, appears to be the greatest frequency a superintendent should attempt if he or she is concerned about turfgrass quality and soil compaction. It is also essential to note, as mentioned earlier, that the research greens that were rolled at a frequency of three times per week were on a frequent sand topdressing program. In addition to considering a safe season-long frequency, it is important to address the impact of season-long lightweight rolling on green speed.

Lightweight Rollers and Green Speed

Most studies on lightweight rolling have considered the immediate (day of rolling) and residual (days after rolling) effect of this cultural practice on green speed. All studies on season-long lightweight green rolling agree that rolling noticeably increases green speed on the day rolling is applied. Understandably, the amount of increase varies from day to day, but, in general, nonrolled plots average approximately 1 foot shorter ball roll distance as compared with rolled plots on the day rolling treatments are applied.

The duration of the effects of lightweight rolling on green speed is not as clear, as several studies report that the residual effects last as long as 48 hours and others conclude that the increase in green speed lasts less than 24 hours. In the search for clear answers to help in the management of green speed, it is important to understand the possible reasons for these discrepancies.

Both the NCSU and MSU studies (and several others) reported that lightweight rolling significantly increased green speed for as long as 48 hours (i.e., the day plots were rolled and the following two days). The key word here is *significantly*. In green speed research, the data (numbers) is normally generated with a Stimpmeter and the measurements are entered into a statistical computer program. Through a series of calculations, the computer program determines whether the findings are *statistically significant* based on variability (differences in green speed) from plot to plot. In regard to studies that have reported statistically significant increases in green speed lasting up to three days, the difference between rolled and nonrolled plots is normally 3 inches or less 48 hours after rolling. The fact that the findings are significant attests to the little variability between the plots and that sound research methods were being practiced. However, because the average golfer cannot detect differences in green speed of 6 inches or less, the findings remain statistically significant but have no realistic application in developing a green speed management strategy.

The majority of lightweight rolling studies have concluded that the day after rolling, the green speed increase attributed to rolling is still greater than 6 inches. This information is used to form a general rule of thumb, that lightweight rolling leads to a noticeable increase in green speed the day of, and the day following, a rolling treatment.

However, the PSU study concluded that the increase in green speed attributed to rolling lasted no more than one day. Why did the PSU study show less residual green speed after rolling than the MSU and NCSU studies? Was this result due to the different types of rollers used at the sites? Did it have something to do with the different rolling frequencies, or was there perhaps something else that was different about the PSU site? The answer to these questions eluded us for several years, but the most recently performed lightweight rolling study may hold the answers, as well as provide another safe frequency for rolling a green.

Research on Various Types of Lightweight Rollers

Although Hutchinson's 1906 definition of light rollers is still applicable to homemade pull-behind units, it clearly does not cover today's factory-manufactured (or dedicated) lightweight rollers. Dedicated lightweight rollers come in a variety of shapes, sizes, and weights. The only similarity between many of them is that they are manufactured with the intended purpose of rolling golf course greens.

In 2002, MSU initiated a lightweight green rolling study to determine whether there were any differences in green speed caused by the various types of rollers currently on the market. The study was performed on a Providence creeping bentgrass green mowed six days per week at 0.125 inch with a Toro walk-behind mower. The root zone fit USGA construction methods, and the site was sand topdressed every two weeks for the duration of the study. Nitrogen inputs were minimal, with the plots receiving 0.10 pounds N per 1000 square feet foliar application every two weeks during the season.

During preparation of the experiment, it became apparent that there remained one important rolling frequency that deserved consideration. Because past research had concluded that lightweight rolling four days a week could produce detrimental effects on the turfgrass and underlying root zone and that rolling three times per week was safe (given that the greens were on a topdressing program), it was decided to roll every other day throughout the season. With that frequency, greens were rolled three times one week and four the next on an alternating basis throughout the season. In addition, given our rule of thumb that lightweight rolling noticeably increases green speed the day of and the day following the rolling treatment, it was expected that an every-other-day frequency would lead to noticeably increased green speeds every day of the week.

There were five different rollers utilized in the study, representing the main types of lightweight rollers on the market (Figure 9-3). Included in the study were the True-Surface Vibratory Roller and four sidewinder units, which included the Salsco and Smithco units, each having two rollers, the DMI Speed Roller with three rollers, and the Tru-Turf Slice and Roll, which has four rollers. Also included in the study were a nonrolled check plot that was mowed six days per week and another nonrolled plot that was double cut six days per week.

FIGURE 9-3. *A number of lightweight rollers on the market come in a variety of styles for transport and use. Pictured from left to right are the True-Surface Vibratory Roller and the sidewinder models, which include Smithco, Salsco, DMI Speed Roller, and the True-Turf Slice and Roll.*

For the first two weeks of the study, Stimpmeter measurements were obtained from the plots nearly every day. On the day plots were rolled, every lightweight roller noticeably and significantly increased green speed, as compared with that of the nonrolled check plots. However, the day after rolling, there was no difference in green speed between any of the rolled and nonrolled plots. These findings were similar to the finding of the PSU study. Perplexed by the results, we searched for a possible cause for the lack of residual green speed, and with a soil probe, discovered an excessive amount of thatch (approximately 1 inch thick) underlying the study's turf.

Obviously, the sponginess caused by an excessive thatch layer could have an effect on the residual green speed attributed to lightweight rolling. Therefore, the site was put on an aggressive thatch reduction program, and as the thatch diminished (over several months), the residual green speed attributed to lightweight rolling increased. In regard to this observation, I had a conversation with George Hamilton of PSU and discussed the MSU findings with him. George acknowledged that his lightweight rolling plots at PSU may also have had a considerable amount of thatch, and we reasoned that thatch thickness could certainly have an impact on residual green speed duration resulting from lightweight rolling.

Granted, on the MSU plots, there was 1 inch of thatch, which would be considered excessive on an actual golf course putting green. As the thatch was reduced to an approximate ½-inch thickness, the residual green speed attributed to lightweight rolling lasted for two days.

Table 9-1 shows the annual average increases in green speed attributed to the different rollers and double cutting on the day plots were rolled and on the day following the rolling treatment. Lowercase letters are included to indicate statistical significance. The average increases followed by the same lowercase letter in each column are not significantly different (that is, they are considered to be equal). These lowercase letters have no meaning going from left to right in the table, but are meaningful only in each column.

In comparing the season averages of 2002 to 2003 on the day plots were rolled, notice that every rolling treatment varied by no more than

TABLE 9-1

Annual Average Increases in Green Speed (in Inches) Attributed to Various Lightweight Rollers and Double Cutting, as Compared with a Daily Mowed Check on Providence Creeping Bentgrass Plots on the Day of and the Day Following Lightweight Rolling Treatments at the Hancock Turfgrass Research Center, East Lansing, Michigan, 2002-2003

Treatment		2002 Season Averages		2003 Season Averages	
		Day Rolled	Day after Roll	Day Rolled	Day after Roll
Check	Daily	e	d	e	c
Double Cut	Daily	10″ d	8″ a	11″ d	12″ a
Speed Roller	EOD	20″ a	7″ ab	20″ a	9″ b
Salsco	EOD	15″ bc	5″ abc	16″ ab	10″ ab
Slice and Roll	EOD	17″ ab	4″ bc	16″ ab	8″ b
True-Surface	EOD	14″ c	3″ c	13″ cd	7″ b
Smithco	EOD	16″ bc	6″ ab	15″ bc	9″ b
Significance		***	***	***	***

All plots were mowed six days per week at a 0.125 inch cutting height.
EOD plots were rolled every other day, thus three days one week, followed by four days the next.
*** Significant 0.001. Means in columns followed by the same letter are not significantly different at the 5% level using the means separation test.

1 inch. For example, notice that the Speed Roller increased green speed 20 inches on the day plots were rolled in 2002 and 2003 and, similarly, the True-Surface Vibratory Roller increased green speed by 14 inches in 2002 and 13 inches in 2003. Clearly, both are noticeable accelerations in green speed.

For the day following the rolling treatment, all the lightweight rollers included in the study significantly increased green speed in both 2002 and 2003, as compared with that of the check plot. However, although all the data was statistically significant in 2002, only the Speed Roller and the Smithco roller averaged an increase in green speed that could possibly be detected by the average golfer. As mentioned earlier, the lack of residual green speed in 2002 was attributed to a 1-inch thatch layer. As the thatch thickness was reduced to $\frac{1}{2}$ inch, all rolling treatments resulted in meaningful increases in green speed the day after rolling in 2003. In short, all rollers included in the study increased green speed by more than a foot on the day rolling was applied and retained more than 6 inches of that increase the day after rolling once the thatch was brought under control.

The rule of thumb indicating that superintendents can expect an average increase in green speed of 1 foot on the day greens are rolled is challenged by the results of this study. Clearly, the type of roller used can result in a noticeable difference in green speed on the day the rolling treatment is applied. However, the differences between the rollers and the increase they generate may not be as great as they appear. Investigating the extremes, we find that the Speed Roller resulted in the fastest green speed in both years on the day plots were rolled, whereas the True Surface averaged the lowest increase in green speed of all the rollers in the study. In 2002, there was a 6-inch difference between those two treatments, and in 2003 an average 7-inch difference. Given that all the other lightweight rollers resulted in green speed increases between these extremes, there is little meaningful difference between the roller types and their impact on green speed.

In addition, the day following the rolling treatments in 2003 (when thatch thickness was reduced), there was only a 3-inch difference in green speed between the rolling treatments. Therefore, another point to consider is variability in green speed from day to day. From the data generated, it appears that rollers that create the quickest green speeds on the day they roll the greens also involve the greatest dropoff in speed the following day. Other factors to be taken into account before purchasing a lightweight roller include its ease of operation, maintenance, and transport from green to green, and its other possible uses; the topography of green surrounds and contours; staffing and the budget.

Double cutting six days per week was included in the study to compare and contrast the differences in the two cultural practices and the impact of each on green speed and the turf. Although there were clearly differences in green speed between double cutting and lightweight rolling, it is easiest to conclude that both cultural practices increased green speed significantly and meaningfully. Thus, it can be said that lightweight rolling every other day results in green speed increases similar to those achieved by double cutting every day. The point is that, in many circumstances, it is less labor-intensive and less wear and fewer hours are required on the mower if an every other day lightweight rolling program is followed in place of double cutting every day.

It is noteworthy that the double-cut plots originally resulted in the lowest turfgrass quality because of scalping, which apparently was exacerbated during the second pass when there was a great deal of thatch on the plots. However, the scalping diminished as the thatch thickness decreased, and subsequently double cutting resulted in no reduction in turfgrass quality during the second year of the study. In all, none of the treatments resulted in a decrease in turfgrass color, quality, bulk density (soil compaction), or water infiltration as compared with the results of the nonrolled single-mowed check plot.

From a careful examination of the studies on long-term lightweight rolling, we can make the following observations:

- On native soil bentgrass greens, three times a week is the highest rolling frequency that can confidently be recommended, given that the greens are on a frequent sand topdressing program.

- On predominantly sandy greens, every other day is the highest frequency that can be recommended for rolling, given that the greens are on a frequent sand topdressing program.

- Given points 1 and 2, lightweight rolling should result in no decreases in turfgrass color or quality, no decrease in water infiltration, and no increase in soil compaction.

- Thatch thickness can have a negative impact on residual green speed. From the study, when thatch thickness was between 1 inch and ½ inch in 2002, only two of the rollers (Speed Roller and Smithco Roller) maintained meaningful residual green speed the

101

day after rolling was applied. However, in 2003, as thatch thickness was decreased to ½ inch and below, all rollers included in the study maintained meaningful green speed increases compared to the nonrolled check plot.

- Increases in green speed attributed to lightweight rollers can be expected to be detected by the golfer on the day the greens are rolled and on the day following the rolling treatment, as long as thatch is not too thick.

- Increases in green speed attributed to lightweight rolling every other day will result in greater or similar green speed increases as those produced by double cutting every day.

Lightweight Rolling and Turfgrass Pests

Dollar Spot

Up to this point, we have observed that lightweight rolling every other day can increase green speed every day of the week without causing compaction in the putting green root zone or a diminishment of turfgrass quality. However, we still need to consider the potential for aboveground turfgrass problems associated with continual season-long turf rolling and the pathogens that may invade crushed tissues, resulting in diseased turf (Beard, 1994). The MSU lightweight rolling study was designed to address these concerns and, in many instances, produced surprising results.

Dollar spot is a turfgrass disease, reportedly spread by maintenance equipment that carries the fungal mycelium and infected plant tissue from green to green (Smiley, 1983). If this is true, then it is reasonable to assume that rolling will increase the severity, and/or exacerbate the spread, of this and similar turfgrass diseases. Dollar spot is commonly considered the most important turfgrass disease, and more money is spent on controlling it than on controlling any other disease (Vargas, 1994). Given these details, if rolling increases the spread and/or severity of this disease, it would certainly justify the apprehension of some superintendents regarding this practice.

However, instead of increasing dollar spot severity, lightweight rolling has actually decreased the severity of this disease on research plots that were rolled three times per week. As noted earlier, the MSU study was initiated in 1995, and, through continued funding from the USGA and the Michigan Turfgrass Foundation, the research was allowed to continue through 2000. During the first year, 4 dollar spot outbreaks occurred on the site. None of the dollar spot data from that first year resulted in statistically significant differences. Interestingly, however, the difference in the amount of dollar spot between the rolled and nonrolled plots grew larger with each succeeding dollar spot count. From 1996 to 2000, a total of 16 dollar spot counts were made on the site, and on every occasion lightweight rolling resulted in significantly less dollar spot than occurred on the nonrolled plots (see Figure 9-4).

A conclusive answer to why lightweight rolling three times per week reduces dollar spot is elusive. Williams and Powell (1995) noted that guttation droplets escape from wound exudates and that these droplets are rich in nutrients that pathogens may use during hyphal growth. Release of these exudates may be exacerbated in the early dawn hours because of a combination of the fresh wounds being produced by mowing and the turgor pressure that may be high at this time. Rolling, following an early morning mowing, may remove inoculum with excess clippings that failed to be caught in the mower bucket, and it may also disperse concentrated guttation water, thus reducing the severity of

FIGURE 9-4. *Season-long rolling at a frequency of three times a week resulted in the rolled plots, like the one on the right, having far less dollar spot than nonrolled plots, like the one on the left.*

the disease. However, a dew-removal dollar spot study performed by Williams and Powell suggests that it is unlikely that dew and guttation removal would account for reductions of the magnitude observed on the research plots at MSU.

Another possible reason that rolling reduced dollar spot is that the water-holding capacity of the root zone may have been increased near the surface layer of the soil. This theory is relevant, because Couch and Bloom found low soil moisture to be important in the development of dollar spot and Howard and Smith reported more dollar spot in seasons with less rainfall (Vargas, 1994). Soil moisture release curves obtained from the MSU plots revealed that the putting green root zones that were lightweight rolled did indeed retain slightly more moisture in the predominantly sandier putting green root zones.

A final theory for reduced severity of dollar spot is that rolling may increase phytoalexin production in the plant. Resistance to diseases can be increased by altering plant response to parasitic attack through the synthesis of phytoalexins (Marschner, 1995). Phytoalexins are antimicrobial low-molecular-weight secondary metabolites that are induced to accumulate as a defense response within the plant (Hammerschmidt, 1999). It may be that lightweight rolling three times per week can stress the turfgrass plant just enough to activate phytoalexin accumulation, yet not stress the turf enough to cause decreases in turfgrass quality.

Moss and Broadleaf Weeds

Other intriguing observations were made over the years at the MSU site regarding turfgrass pests and lightweight rolling. In 1996, moss encroachment was observed on the site. The data collected showed significantly less moss growth on the plots that were rolled as compared with the nonrolled plots. In 1998, broadleaf weeds, mainly dandelion and plantain, infested the plots. In October of that year, broadleaf weeds were counted, and as with the moss growth, the plots that were lightweight rolled had significantly fewer broadleaf weeds.

In regard to the moss and broadleaf weed data, it would probably be inaccurate to conclude that lightweight rolling decreased (killed) either of these turfgrass pests. It is more likely that the research greens that were on a lightweight rolling program exhibited greater turfgrass density, which resulted in less favorable conditions for the encroachment of these pests.

Cutworms

In 1996, 1999, and 2000, bird activity was high on the MSU lightweight-rolling site. The increased bird activity coincided with the observation of numerous black cutworms (*Agrotis ipsilon*) on the plots. During those incidents when black cutworms were observed on the site, bird beak intrusion counts were made on the putting greens prior to mowing (Figure 9-5). There were significantly fewer bird beak intrusions on greens that were rolled, with reductions of 56 percent reported on rolled plots in 1996, 59 percent fewer in 1999, and 56 percent fewer in 2000. The precision of the reductions is obviously intriguing.

If we make the assumption that fewer bird beak intrusions were the result of fewer black cutworms, then the question is, why would lightweight rolling result in fewer cutworms? To address that question, we should consider that Potter (1998) reported that black cutworm moths lay nearly all their eggs on the tips of leaf blades and that many survive passage through the mower blades and will hatch later. Considering that debris (excess clippings that miss the bucket) adheres to rollers and is transported off-site, it is conceivable that rolling could have decreased

FIGURE 9-5. *Plots rolled three times a week consistently had fewer bird peck holes when the level of cutworm activity was high.*

105

the number of cutworms by removing the eggs with the excess debris. Golf course architect Peter Lees made a similar observation regarding debris removal in 1918, as he noted, "Another point in using the wooden roller is that it picks up worm casts or other matter lying loose on the surface" (Lees, 1918).

Localized Dry Spot

There was a final interesting observation made regarding lightweight rolling on the MSU plots. Over the years, when heat stress became an issue, it appeared that there were fewer localized dry spots on the greens that received the rolling treatment. Following a rain event in August 2000, irrigation was turned off to allow the plots to dry to permit the development of localized dry spot. When the percentage of localized dry spot on each plot was determined, the plots that were lightweight rolled had fewer localized dry spots than the plots that were not rolled (Figure 9-6).

It may seem counterintuitive that lightweight rolling would decrease the incidence of localized dry spots on the putting surface. Interestingly,

FIGURE 9-6. *Plots rolled three times a week displayed less localized dry spot than neighboring plots that were not rolled.*

an observation on this subject was made decades earlier. In a 1922 article titled "Treatment for Unwatered Greens," Maynard Metcalf noted, "The rolling did the sandy soil good" and "using this treatment upon a clay soil only a light roller should be used, and on such soil the top-dressing used might well be more largely sand." Why would rolling decrease localized dry spot? There are actually two good reasons derived from the data collected at MSU: (1) As previously noted, the greens that were rolled retained more moisture in the soil, and (2) greens that were lightweight rolled had significantly more roots in the topdressing layer as compared with nonrolled plots. Both of these findings could clearly result in less localized dry spot.

I recently had a conversation with a former New Zealand turfgrass manager of bowling green lawns. It is pertinent to point out that lightweight rolling has been a common practice on bowling greens for decades. When he observed the data regarding fewer localized dry spots on greens that were rolled, he smiled and noted that he had always thought rolling reduced the need for irrigation.

Snow Mold

The only negative surface response I have observed in regard to lightweight rolling three times per week (or less) occurred at the MSU site in 1996. In June of that year, plots that were rolled exhibited significantly more *Microdochium* patch as compared with nonrolled plots.

Microdochium patch is also commonly called pink snow mold. The trouble with the name "pink snow mold" is that it implies the disease is a problem only under snow cover; however, it is a major disease without snow cover in regions that have extended periods of cool, wet weather. When the disease occurred in June 1996 on the MSU research plots, it followed an extended period of cool, wet weather.

The occurrence of *Microdochium* patch in June in mid-Michigan is uncommon, and unfortunately there were no other *Microdochium* patch outbreaks that occurred during the rolling season on the plots for the remaining four years of the study. However, it is noteworthy that in the late winter, early spring, or late fall of each year when plots (rolled and nonrolled) displayed pink snow mold symptoms following snow melt, there were never any differences in the amount of disease symptoms that could be attributed to rolling or the lack of it. Therefore, it appears that if lightweight rolling does increase *Microdochium* patch, it is not likely to increase under the cover of snow but more likely during extended periods of cool, wet weather when the greens are being rolled. Why this might occur is not obvious, and clearly more research is needed to address this potential problem.

Conclusions About Lightweight Rolling

The practice of lightweight rolling has long been a controversial subject. Because lightweight rolling is primarily practiced to increase green speed, data regarding the practice did not have to indicate that it alleviated the infestation of any turfgrass pests. Instead, the data just had to indicate that it did increase green speed without significant decreases in turf quality or increases in soil compaction or turfgrass pest to demonstrate that lightweight rolling is a viable cultural practice to help manage green speed.

Given the results of the research conducted on lightweight rollers, it appears that three or four days a week is a safe frequency for rolling greens on a sand topdressing program to avoid compaction and losses in turfgrass quality. As long as thatch thickness is not greater than ½ inch, the data is clear that rolling should result in a noticeable increase in green speed for two days (the day rolled and the day following).

Lightweight rolling at a frequency of three times per week has also resulted in fewer occurrences of dollar spot symptoms, moss, broadleaf weeds, localized dry spot, and bird beak intrusion (and, perhaps, cutworms). However, on one occasion, it did increase *Microdochium* patch. There is still some vital research that must be performed in regard to this cultural practice. We still do not know what effect it has, if any, on *Pythium*, anthracnose, gray leaf spot, and other pests. Undoubtedly, some superintendents will continue to be apprehensive, but just as many will agree with the comments of W. S. Harban when he noted, "I cannot conceive how a perfect putting surface can be developed or maintained without rolling" and "I do not believe in rolling as a mere fad, but do think there are times when it is indispensable to make, keep, and protect a proper turf and surface on greens" (Harban et al., 1922).

One thing certainly seems clear, that lightweight rolling can be an important part of an integrated approach to green speed management.

10

An Integrated Approach to Green Speed Management and Tournament Preparation

*A look at the greens' root zone should show a clean,
consistent profile with deep root penetration.
Unfortunately, that frequently is not the case, particularly
if the green construction is not up to current USGA
recommendations. Previous topdressing practices and old
sod layers also can significantly restrict root depth. Short
roots in greens not yet under heavy tournament stress can
spell disaster during the rigors of championship
maintenance routines.*
PGA TOUR AGRONOMIST JON SCOTT, 1998

The Scenario

When I have consulted with golf courses to assist in enhancement of their green speeds for tournament or everyday play, I have been privy to the cultural management strategies currently employed. Likewise, when major tournaments are hosted by the United States Golf Association (USGA) or the Professional Golfers Association (PGA) Tour, both organizations have agronomists that specialize in preparation of the site several years in advance and are knowledgeable about the cultural practices of the site.

Numerous articles and speakers who address the issue of green speed often conclude by stating, "Green speed management should be part of an integrated program." Although the phrase "integrated approach to green speed management" is vague, it should be understood that it is impossible for anyone to make adjustments to a program without knowing what the program currently entails (Figure 10-1).

This chapter addresses the integrated approach to green speed management. It uses data already considered, as well as other cultural management practices that play a role. As these issues are explored, the complexity of such an approach will become apparent. It is hoped that as you read through the data, you will find information to assist your course's individual needs for everyday play or tournament preparation.

Cultivation

The following query appeared in a "Turf Twister" in the November–December 2003 issue of the *USGA Green Section Record.* "I am the Green Chairman at our course, and the superintendent and I are having a dis-

FIGURE 10-1. *Bob Vavrek of the USGA tells a Golf Association of Michigan audience about the importance of taking an integrated approach to green speed management.*

agreement concerning aeration. Since we are in a cold region where golf is played from late March to early November, I say we only need to aerify once a year. Our superintendent says twice with large tines is necessary. Is the spring aeration needed when we have no play during the winter?"

Core cultivation is clearly the most contentious cultural management practice a superintendent employs. Traditionally, putting greens are core cultivated once or twice a year, and some advocate that newer bent and Bermudagrass cultivar greens be core cultivated three times per year (Figure 10-2 and Figure 10-3).

Ed Fischer, CGCS, of the Old Elm Club in Libertyville, Illinois, spoke for many a superintendent and golfer alike when he noted, in regard to core cultivation, "It's labor intensive, and the golfers are never happy afterwards" (Ostmeyer, 2003). Partially for these reasons, some superintendents have implemented other cultural management strategies that have allowed them to forgo core cultivation on their greens for years.

FIGURE 10-2. *Thatch and layering resulting from inconsistent topdressing can pose problems when you are trying to accelerate green speeds for a tournament.*

FIGURE 10-3. *Aggressive cultural practices are often necessary to maintain a healthy root zone and are a key part of the integrated approach to putting green management. (Images courtesy of Matt Taylor, CGCS Royal Poinciana Golf Club, Florida)*

In regard to green speed, the holes left on the putting surface following core cultivation, either filled or unfilled, can disrupt the speed and the line of a putt. In the short term, how much does core cultivation actually disrupt the green speed and what can be done to alleviate this disruption as soon as possible? Several studies and their findings can be instructive.

In 2003, Michigan State University (MSU) performed a core cultivation study with ¼-inch tines. Prior to backfilling the holes with sand, green speed measurements were obtained. The result was that the aerified plots were 1 foot 3 inches slower than the nonaerified plots, clearly a significant decrease in speed.

In 1981, Clark Throssell performed core cultivation studies with ¼-inch and ½-inch tines, applying two different amounts of topdressing to the holes. Green speed was measured with a Stimpmeter every other day for 20 days following the treatments. As would be expected, aerification reduced green speed, as Clark noted, "A greater speed reduction occurred on plots aerified with ½-inch tines than those aerified with ¼-inch tines," but, just as important, "as the rate of topdressing increased, the difference between aerification treatments decreased" (Throssell, 1981).

Stahnke and Beard corroborated Throssell findings, as they reported that coring reduced green speed by 7 percent, but "after applying sand topdressing, the ball was again rolled over these plots, and an 8 percent increase in length of ball roll occurred compared to the coring alone." In other words, the practice of sand topdressing following the core culti-vation "increased the green surface quality to the original playing speed existing before the area was cored" (Stahnke and Beard, 1981).

The message is clear: Properly backfilling the holes with an appropriate topdressing material and smoothing the surface can quickly counteract the negative impact of core cultivation on green speed. A newer approach many superintendents have adopted is to use a roller following core cultivation. In the case of deep-tine aerification, lightweight rolling over the uplifted turf around the holes reduces scalping and facilitates ball roll.

It can also be advantageous to apply a granular fertilization treatment a week or two before core cultivation to enhance turf growth to cover the holes. As noted in Chapter 8, some superintendents have shied away from granular applications of fertilizer, but the data is clear that granular applications can have beneficial effects on the turf without reducing green speed. Sean O'Connor, CGCS, of the Forest Akers Golf Course in East Lansing, Michigan, likes to use his vibratory roller after applying an or-ganic granular fertilizer. Sean says he can "actually see the granules move below the surface" and "fewer fertilizer granules end up on the mower rollers" and in the bucket the next day.

Another important point is the relevance of taking green speed mea-surements on the same green several days prior to and following core cultivation. These measurements can be included in a spreadsheet or graph to be used at green committee meetings. In Chapter 3, I advocate the determination of the ideal green speed and stress the importance of taking green speed measurements on at least one putting green daily. Dur-ing operations such as core cultivation, this simple daily task demonstrates to the clientele that the superintendent is concerned about green speed and is taking measures to control it.

So far, we have addressed only the immediate impact of core cultiva-tion on green speed. What about its long-term effects? Core cultivation is often sold to the golfer as a means of reducing compaction and the buildup of thatch/organic matter or of increasing water and oxygen exchange. In some instances, it may be advantageous to inform golfers that core cultivation is a key part of an integrated approach to green speed management, that core cultivation can actually lead to enhanced green speeds.

When thatch/organic matter is allowed to build up, the golf ball will sink (albeit imperceptibly) into the putting surface, which results in a slower green speed. We have already demonstrated that thatch buildup has negative consequences for the residual green speed attributed to lightweight rolling. Therefore, keeping thatch from becoming a problem promotes better green speed uniformity from day to day, especially on greens that are rolled every other day. Furthermore, double cutting on wet greens with too much thatch leads to scalping, and under these circumstances double cutting may actually decrease green speed. Even if scalping does not decrease the green speed, it may affect the line of the putt as the ball rolls, and scalped turf is never aesthetically pleasing.

Thus, although core cultivation does have an immediate negative impact on green speed, with good equipment and other sound cultural practices the decrease in speed can be short-lived. The practice may best be sold to a club's members as part of an integrated approach to green speed management.

As noted earlier, some superintendents have opted not to core cultivate as part of their annual greens management programs. Instead, most have taken other precautionary steps to control thatch/organic matter buildup or enhance water infiltration and oxygen exchange. These programs include frequent sand topdressing, verticutting, and water or air injection (Figure 10-4).

Topdressing

In the late 1800s, Tom Morris mistakenly tipped a wheelbarrow full of sand onto a green he was having difficulty maintaining. Rather than shoveling the sand back into the wheelbarrow, he chose to spread it across the green. Later, Tom noticed that the health of the grass had been restored, and the practice of sand topdressing greens was born (Labbance and Witteveen, 2002) (Figure 10-5).

(a)

(b)

FIGURE 10-4 (a, b). *John Rogers III informs his students about the importance of good cultural practices in maintaining a green's root zone. The soil profile is taken from a putting green that had not been core aerified in 20 years because of a dedicated sand topdressing and vertical mowing management program.*

FIGURE 10-5. *Sand topdressing techniques have come a long way since Tom Morris, by accident, tipped over a wheelbarrow of sand on one of his greens. (Images courtesy of Matt Taylor, CGCS Royal Poinciana Golf Club, Florida)*

In 1906, Gilbert Beale wrote of the practice: "Sea-sand is frequently used as a dressing for putting greens resting upon stiff soils, with the twofold object of firming-up the surface and fining-down too vigorous growth of grass" (Hutchinson, 1906). Though topdressing has been around for a long time, the frequency of the application has changed. Traditionally, many courses topdressed only once or twice a year following core cultivation. In the 1970s, when mower bedknife thickness decreased and mowing heights were lowered, the frequency of sand topdressing every three weeks became popular to help keep the surface smooth. Today, some superintendents lightly "dust" their greens with kiln-dried sand applied with a fertilizer spreader.

The results of research on green speed and topdressing are mixed. In 1998, research was conducted with various topdressing mixtures applied at different frequencies. Plots were either cored and topdressed twice a year or lightly topdressed every three weeks without coring. During the study, only a couple of green speed measurements were obtained, and they showed no meaningful effect on green speed attributed to the different topdressing programs (Rieke et al., 1988). It was also noted that the plots that were cored previous to sand application had lower organic matter contents than most of the other plots that were not cored.

Clark Throssell performed green speed–topdressing research and applied topdressing material at two different rates. Throssell concluded that a decrease in speed for eight days should be anticipated following either a light or a heavy topdressing treatment. However, as the topdressing gets worked into the turf or is removed by mowing, the green speed will begin to increase on the topdressed plots. Throssell noted that after eight days, "until the termination of the experiment, speed was greater on the topdressing treated plots than the non-topdressed checks even though the speed on the check plots increased throughout the duration of the experiment" (Throssel, 1981). Clearly, Throssel has made many important contributions to green speed issues, and I have always thought that his topdressing information is an important consideration in regard to tournament preparation. His work clearly suggests that in preparation for a golf tournament, it is advisable to topdress at least eight days before the tournament to get the maximum benefit from the topdressing application.

Many golfers (and perhaps some superintendents) refuse to accept the idea that green speed will initially be decreased following a sand topdressing application. It should be noted that many golf courses use alternative mowers with old bedknives and reels for several days following a sand topdressing application. When this is done, the greens are probably not getting cut as tightly as usual, and therefore the decreased cutting quality due to dull blades could result in the decreased green speed attributed to sand topdressing. Furthermore, golf courses that do not change mowers can end up with extremely dull bedknives and reels because of the topdressing material, which also results in a diminished quality of cut that can decrease green speed.

Under most circumstances, it appears that topdressing will increase green speed after some initial decline. Therefore, when topdressing is used, it is important to find a way to facilitate the incorporation of the topdressing material below the turfgrass canopy. Evidently, this problem was the reason for some superintendents using a light "dusting" with a kiln-dried sand every week. However, the dusting method of application is not practical for most superintendents, and the importance of uniform distribution with good drag mats and/or brushes cannot be overemphasized.

A newer approach with which some superintendents are evidently having success is the use of vibratory rollers following a sand topdressing application. The idea is that the vibratory action of the roller helps to smooth the surface and alleviate the bridging associated with brushing or dragging and, under some circumstances, may help to facilitate the movement of sand grains below the turfgrass canopy. In 2002, MSU performed a preliminary vibratory rolling–topdressing study on the nursery green at the Forest Akers Golf Course. As a result, the plots that were vibratory rolled after sand topdressing had 30 percent less sand in the mower buckets the next day as compared with the plots that were drag-matted in. There are many variables that can affect the success or failure of this method and the approach needs to be researched in greater detail, but it is noteworthy in that some superintendents are happy with the results they have achieved.

From a survey of 107 golf courses in Nebraska and South Dakota from 1994 to 1996, Ann Rist and Roch Gaussoin concluded, "Topdressing eight times per year will increase ball-roll distance at a nitrogen rate of 0.33 pounds per 1,000 square feet per month. But at greater nitrogen rates, only two topdressings per year are needed to get maximum ball-roll distance." Results from the survey also indicated, "As topdressing and verticutting frequency increased, ball-roll distance decreased." The implication is that "topdressing and verticutting 16 to 20 times per year requires that those processes be done every seven to 10 days. This time interval may not allow the surface to get back to smooth putting conditions" (Rist and Gaussoin, 1997).

If we consider all the different frequencies, methods, and amounts of material applied through various topdressing programs, it should become obvious that almost any blanket statement made about topdressing and green speed is going to be inaccurate. Under most circumstances, it is safe to assume that topdressing will enhance green speed, but the amount of time between the application and incorporation of the material and the enhancement of the green speed will ultimately be determined by the aforementioned variables.

A most important point is that "greens that are not topdressed become thatchy and puffy, and can result in scalping and shorter ball-roll distances" (Streich and Gaussoin, 2000). Therefore, topdressing, like core cultivation, may best be thought of as a preventive measure to stop thatch/organic matter buildup, which will ultimately decrease green speed. The only way to be certain of the immediate effect of topdressing on the speed of your greens is to take green speed measurements several days prior to and following the application of the topdressing material.

Vertical Mowing and Grooming

A common assumption is that the more upright the turfgrass growth, the greater the green speed, or in other words, green speed should be enhanced when the ball rolls across the leaf tips instead of the flat leaf blades. In the introduction to his research paper on vertical mowing Salaiz noted, "Light vertical mowing is expected to enhance putting green speed by controlling turfgrass grain and increasing surface smoothness, since vertical blades only penetrate the turfgrass canopy." In this study Salaiz mowed plots vertically at frequencies of none, one, and two times per month, with knifes spaced ½ inch (13 millimeters) apart, set to a depth so that the vertical knives entered the canopy surface only. The results: "Vertical mowing frequency treatments had no effect on ball roll distance under the conditions of this study" (Salaiz et al., 1995).

Clark Throssell investigated the effects of two different vertical mowing treatments on green speed. One treatment he described as a light verticutting, and the other as groove verticutting to a ⅛-inch depth. After the treatments were applied, Clark noted, "The light verticutting and the nonverticut check were not significantly different," but the "groove verticutting" resulted in significantly less green speed than the light verticutting and the nonverticutting check (Throssel, 1981).

In 1983 and 1984, Langlois performed vertical mowing studies on plots mowed at 0.188- and 0.125-inch heights of cut. He reported that "weekly light verticutting increased speed 0.5 to 1.2 ft on plots mowed at" the higher cutting height for both years of the study. Similar results occurred at the 0.125-inch mowing height in the first year of the study but not during the second year (Langlois, 1985).

Thus, the research has variously shown that vertical mowing on putting greens will decrease, increase, or have no impact on green speed (Figure 10-6). Evidently, other factors must come into play, such as friction, the force that changes movement as a result of surface-to-surface contact. Friction is increased when two coarse surfaces are in contact with each other. Therefore, there is less friction when one surface is smooth and the other is coarse, and even less friction is created between two smooth

FIGURE 10-6. *Many factors determine whether a vertical mowing program increases, decreases, or has no immediate effect on green speed. However, in the long term, thatch and organic matter control is an important part of taking control of green speed. (Images courtesy of Matt Taylor, CGCS Royal Poinciana Golf Club, Florida)*

surfaces. In regard to green speed, the smoother the putting surface, the less friction between the ball and the putting surface.

Results from the aforementioned studies indicate that vertical mowing can either increase or decrease the smoothness of the surface, depending on several factors. It seems intuitive that with a wider and deeper "tine" penetration, a less smooth, or a coarser, surface would be created and a temporary reduction in green speed would result.

Anne Rist and Roch Gaussoin (1997) made some interesting observations on verticutting and grooming in regard to the golf course surveys they collected:

- Frequent verticutting would increase ball-roll distances only when nitrogen rates are less than 0.40 pound per 1,000 sq. ft per month.

- When nitrogen rate exceeded 0.70 pound per 1,000 square feet per month, the ball-roll response was reversed and maximum ball-roll distance was achieved when verticutting was not done.

- Results indicate that grooming is an important practice only at mowing heights less than 0.146 inch. Above this mowing height no significant ball-roll distance is gained from grooming.

- The two common mowing heights that would benefit from grooming are 0.125 and 0.141 inch. But at these two mowing heights, golfers wouldn't detect an increase in ball roll unless grooming occurs more than four times per week.

- Grooming can actually cause a significant decrease in ball-roll distance when mowing heights are greater than 0.177 inch or at nitrogen rates less than 0.82 pound per 1,000 square feet per month.

Rist and Gaussoin's work clearly demonstrates the complexity involved in creating a smooth surface to facilitate green speed.

Because there are numerous ways to core cultivate, topdress and fill in the holes, incorporate a topdressing material below the turfgrass canopy, and verticut, it is improbable that research can give a superintendent a definite answer as to how these practices immediately affect the green speed on his or her greens. However, it should always be remembered that these practices are all performed to prevent the buildup of thatch/organic matter, which makes them an important part of the integrated approach to green speed management.

Water and Air Injection Cultivation

In any integrated approach to green speed management, cultivation via water and/or air injection deserves attention. These two cultural practices should not be considered a replacement for core cultivation, because neither decreases thatch/organic matter. However, research has shown that both water and air injection can increase water infiltration. Therefore, superintendents who have shied away from establishing annual core cultivation programs can and do incorporate these practices in concert with sand topdressing and vertical mowing, inasmuch as both can decrease the development of thatch/organic matter.

The HydroJect is the most well-researched means of water injection cultivation (WIC). It utilizes a 5000-psi water blast to help relieve compaction and aerify soil. An original benefit of WIC was that it did not disrupt the soil surface as traditional core cultivation did.

The HydroJect has two large rollers that shoulder the weight of the unit while it is injecting the water. These rollers apparently perform like traditional green-rolling units. In research plots at Michigan State University, the HydroJect treatment resulted in increased green speed averaging approximately 6 inches (Karcher et al., 1996). The golfer may not notice this increase in speed, but the point is that it does not *decrease* green speed as it provides benefits to the putting surface and soil.

How often should WIC be practiced? My experience with a HydroJect suggests that the maximum benefits are realized with regular use. I envision a program in which every other Monday greens receive water injection in place of a lightweight rolling. Clearly, this is too-labor intensive for many golf courses, but there are potential benefits, such as reduced moisture stress and a decrease in earthworm castings.

Several studies performed at Michigan State University included plots that received weekly WIC treatments and plots that received no WIC treatments. Irrigation was withheld from one of these studies to encourage localized dry spot. The results were obvious; the WIC-treated plots had higher moisture contents and fewer localized dry spots (see Figure 10-7). Similar results have been found on other sites; Gibbs noted the benefit of "the HydroJect, when used in conjunction with wetting agent, in providing outstanding control of dry patch in the sand-based root zones" (Gibbs et al., 2000). Since irrigation is often minimized in an effort to enhance green speed cultural practices like the HydroJect and the use of wetting agents can be of considerable benefit in decreasing the incidence of localized dry spots.

FIGURE 10-7. *Regular water injection cultivation (with and without wetting agents) has been shown to alleviate localized dry spot.*

Doug Karcher also observed fewer earthworm castings on plots that received biweekly WIC treatments. He attributed the earthworm control to "increased amounts of macropores so the earthworms can cast below the turfgrass surface during periods of heavy rainfall. This scenario results in reduced amounts of casting on the turfgrass surface while maintaining the beneficial burrowing activities of the earthworms (Karcher et al., 1996).

In regard to air injection cultivation (AIC), there are several types of equipment on the market. Some can inject Styrofoam pellets, sand, or other types of amendments with air-pressurized blasts. There is not a great deal of documentation on AIC at this time. However, in the fall of 2003, we did perform a one-day study at MSU with a unit that injects between 60 and 70 pounds of air (Figure 10-8). The probes that inject the air are 2 feet apart and can penetrate as deep as 12 inches. As a result of the air injection, we did see enhanced water infiltration two weeks after treat-

FIGURE 10-8. *Air injection cultivation treatments can increase water infiltration.*

ment. Immediately after treatment, there was no difference in green speed between plots that received AIC and those that did not.

Plant Growth Regulators

I am a strong advocate of plant growth regulators (PGRs) as part of an integrated approach to green speed management, but I cringe every time I hear someone say that he or she uses PGRs to increase green speed.

The first turfgrass research I ever performed was in 1991 on PennLinks creeping bentgrass plots, mowed at three different cutting heights (0.188, 0.157, and 0.125 inch) and receiving two different types of PGRs (florprimidol and paclobutrazol); both PGRs were applied at two different rates every 30 days. Green speed measurements were obtained 14 times during the course of the study, and measurements at only four of the dates showed significant differences. On those four dates, there was an increase in green speed due to PGR treatment at the two higher cutting heights, but we could not duplicate these findings the next two years (Rogers et al, 1992).

A similar study took place in North Carolina, with the PGRs paclobutrazol and trinexapac-ethyl applied monthly from April to December on creeping bentgrass plots mowed at heights of 0.188, 0.157, and 0.125 inch. Green speed measurements were recorded monthly, showing that PGRs had no effect on putting green speed (Yelverton, 1998).

There are numerous other studies that could be cited, and in some cases we could find that "7 to 14 days after application," a PGR increased green speed. It should also be noted that there are limitless possibilities of rates and nitrogen treatments that may produce an increase in green speed attributed to a particular PGR. However, the data suggests nothing worth counting on at this time.

Chapter 8 discussed a fertility study that incorporated Primo Maxx (trinexapac-ethyl) applications at one-third the labeled rate every 10 days and at the labeled rate every 30 days. The results indicated no predictable increases in green speed attributed to the PGR application. Far more important, however, was the finding that the PGR did increase the turfgrass quality, especially on plots with the lowest nitrogen rates.

So, although I may cringe when I hear someone say he or she uses PGRs to increase green speed, I have decided that what that person was really implying was that PGRs improved turfgrass color and quality when used in conjunction with lower mowing heights and nitrogen rates, which results in increased green speed.

In addition, because several fairway studies have shown hastened divot recovery with PGRs, it may be fair to assume that PGRs may also hasten cup, ball mark, and foot traffic recovery on the putting surface. The enhanced leaf elongation and color of turfgrass produced by trinexapac-ethyl makes it a significant piece of the integrated approach to green speed management.

It is certainly noteworthy that numerous golf courses use PGRs for seed head suppression of *Poa annua* on their putting greens. This application for PGRs most likely does result in an increase in green speed, but there is no study in the literature that validates this assumption.

Irrigation

Histosols are defined as organic soils that have organic soil materials in more than half of the upper 80 centimeters (approximately 30 inches). They develop where the soil is saturated continuously for at least one month each year. Although they are found around the world, the Florida Everglades is one of the most famous Histosol sites. When Histosols are drained, oxygen is introduced, decomposition is enhanced, and subsidence occurs as organic matter decomposes (Foth, 1978). The point is that wetter soils are more apt to accumulate organic matter, and drying them results in a decrease of organic matter.

In my class on golf turf irrigation, I give a quiz early in the semester regarding a subject we have yet to cover. The question is, "Name five negative consequences of overirrigated turf and five negative consequences of underirrigated turf." When grading the quizzes, I invariably find that almost every student has named five negative consequences of overirrigated turf but almost none have named five of underirrigated turf. I tabulate the results and distribute them for conversation during the next class period. We generally end up with about 20 negative consequences of overirrigated turf, 7 to 8 negative consequences of underirrigated turf, and some consequences we place in both categories. The students thus prove to themselves that overirrigated turf creates far more ominous turfgrass problems than underirrigated turf.

A consideration of three studies of the effect of irrigation on green speed can be helpful. Following a rain event in August of 2002, we initiated an irrigation–green speed study at the Hancock Turfgrass Research Center at MSU. Treatments included no irrigation, $1/10$ inch of irrigation, and $1/4$ inch of irrigation. Plots that received the $1/4$-inch irrigation had standing water on them, forcing us to postpone the morning mowing until the water subsided. The study ran for only two successive days because it began raining again. However, on the two days when green speed measurements were taken, there were no significant differences between the treatments in regard to green speed.

In July 1983, an irrigation–green speed study was performed at Pennsylvania State University on Penneagle creeping bentgrass plots mowed at 0.125 inch. The treatments consisted of irrigation applied to provide surface saturation and the syringing of nonwatered plots to sustain the grass. The researchers reported, "The greenspeed on the nonwatered plots never exceeded the watered by more than 4 inches over an eight-day period" (Duich and Langlois, 1985).

In England, an irrigation–green speed study was performed on three different root zone construction types (sand, soil, and USGA). The irrigation treatments were 75 percent, 100 percent, and 125 percent replacement of evapotranspiration (ET) losses in 1990. There was a "failure of the irrigation treatments to induce any noticeable responses" (Lodge and Baker, 1991), so the irrigation treatments were changed to 60 percent, 100 percent, and 140 percent of ET losses in 1991 and 1992. The data reported was not generated with a Stimpmeter, but of the "distance traveled by the balls after impact" with a simulated 5-iron. Results of the study were that the sand root zone showed the least significant difference in ball roll due to irrigation treatments, followed by the USGA and the soil root zones.

What is most intriguing about the study is that on the one occasion of statistical significance on the sand construction green, the longest ball roll distance was achieved with the highest irrigation rate. However, when significant differences were obtained on the USGA and soil construction types, the longest ball roll distances were obtained in plots with the lowest irrigation rates. Fortunately, surface hardness measurements were also obtained from the plots, and it was found that "increased irrigation rate produced harder surfaces on the sand construction and softer surfaces on the USGA and soil construction." It is quite interesting that from these results the researchers concluded, "If irrigation management were to be used to alter ball behavior on a green, these data would suggest that it is necessary to understand the effects of irrigation on green hardness" (Lodge, 1992).

Some may ask, "Then is it true that as the surface dries out there will not be an increase in green speed?" No, that is not what the data implies at all. It is important here not to confuse two different issues.

The obvious implication of the first two irrigation studies is that changes in irrigation practices should not be expected to result in immediate differences in green speed. The third study suggests that different root zones should be expected to react differently under different irrigation regimes and that the firmness of the playing surface should be expected to have a greater impact on green speed than the moisture content in the root zone.

What must be understood is that none of the research studies mentioned here reported surface moisture measurements. If they had, would we really expect to see substantial differences? My study lasted only two days, and once the standing water on the most heavily irrigated plots infiltrated into the soil, there was really no reason to expect differences in the surface moisture. None of the studies mentioned that some plots were at the wilting point and the others lush and succulent.

I hypothesize that long-term irrigation studies would eventually result in differences in green speed and that the differences would coincide with increases in thatch, organic matter, and black layer development on plots receiving the highest rates of irrigation. In addition, if the plots with the lowest irrigation rates exhibited excessive wilting, those plots would probably exhibit faster green speeds than nonwilted plots. However, on test plots receiving different amounts of irrigation with similar thatch/organic matter contents, on which wilting does not occur, there is really no reason to expect differences in green speed. Therefore, in the short term, there is no reason to expect that various irrigation practices would result in significant differences in green speed. After all, how far below the putting surface should we expect moisture to affect green speed?

Irrigation practices as part of an integrated approach to green speed management should be balanced between applying irrigation at rates conducive to keeping the plants satisfied but not so great as to encourage thatch/organic matter/black layer development.

Tournament Preparation

Although green speed is a daily concern for some superintendents, it is likely that the majority of golf course superintendents most often become concerned about green speed during a club invitational or other important events (Figure 10-9). For this reason, the subject of tournament preparation could warrant its own chapter. However, I have included it in this chapter because:

It is difficult, if not impossible, to make recommendations for tournament preparations without knowing what the current management practices are at a specific site.

Putting surfaces that have thatch/organic matter under control are not only more apt to produce greater green speeds but are also less apt to experience difficulties when short-term management strategies are employed to increase green speed for a tournament. In preparing for a club championship, additional cultural practices such as double cutting or grooming are often added in an effort to increase the green speed. When double cutting is haphazardly introduced, without taking thatch thickness into consideration, scalping often occurs. Therefore, because most of this chapter deals with cultural practices that focus on thatch/organic matter as part of an integrated approach to green speed management, tournament preparation is logically discussed here.

FIGURE 10-9. *Golf course superintendents who want to increase their green speeds for club tournaments and/or special outings are well advised to take proper care of their putting green root zones.*

The superintendent of any course in the United States that hosts a professional tournament will have the USGA or PGA Tour agronomist to help chart a path to green speed success for the event. Therefore, this discussion of tournament preparation refers to preparation for a club championship, member guest, or an important event at a particular course. The member-guest tournament is considered the most or second most important golf outing at the majority of private country clubs. During this annual event, a member of the country club is allowed to invite a guest to play at the course. With that said, it should be clear that the golf course must be in perfect condition for that day and that green speeds are generally elevated for member bragging rights to their guests.

As mentioned in Chapter 3, Mike Morris, CGCS, of Crystal Downs Country Club and his green committee determined the ideal green speed of their golf course through a series of golfer surveys. As a result of their efforts, the green committee informed Mike that it was no longer necessary to increase green speeds on the course for tournament play. Clearly, every golf course that takes time to determine its ideal green speed would not come to the same decision; however, once a superintendent and a green committee have located the ideal green speed, why would they vary from it?

Sand Topdressing

As discussed previously, there are many ways to topdress greens. On golf courses that topdress every two or three weeks throughout the season, the data strongly suggests that the last topdressing prior to a tournament should be applied at least eight days before the tournament for maximum green speed enhancement. Long-term planning with a calendar is advised.

Nitrogen Fertilization

The data strongly suggests that withholding a nitrogen fertilizer application for a short period of time prior to a tournament will not result in a noticeable increase in green speed. The turfgrass quality and its ability to recuperate must always be considered. Once you have determined the fertilization requirements for your golf course that take into consideration turfgrass quality, recuperative potential, and green speed, be consistent in using them as a guide.

Mowing Height Reduction

I cannot advocate reducing mowing height prior to a club tournament or event. PGA Tour agronomist Jon Scott wrote, "It would be a big mistake to wait until a few weeks before the event to start lowering the height of cut. Almost invariably this results in severe scalping and places undue stress on the turf before the tournament begins" (Scott, 1998). From the data presented in Chapter 7, we can also infer that many times mowing heights are dropped without any meaningful increase in green speed.

Double Cutting

This is where the "integrated approach" to green speed management really comes into play. If double cutting is not part of your routine practice, be cognizant of your thatch/mat layer. If it is more than ½ inch thick, be extremely cautious, especially if there is excessive moisture in the layer due to rain, irrigation, high humidity, or any combination of these, because scalping may result. Play it safe and double cut your nursery or portions of a chipping or putting green several weeks before the event as a check (if they are on the same maintenance schedule and have similar underlying profiles). Once you feel comfortable that the practice is safe for the greens, double cutting should begin a week to several days prior to the tournament to achieve the maximum green speed benefit.

Rolling

For golf courses that do not roll on a regular basis, rolling should be performed every other day a week or two before the event. Plan it into the schedule so that rolling will take place on the day of the event. It is important to note that the data suggests that lightweight rolling every day for a short time (two weeks) should not result in any negative effects on the turfgrass plant or its underlying root zone. Therefore, golf courses that routinely lightweight roll every other day will most likely experience a noticeable increase in green speed if rolling is performed every day for a week or two prior to and through the duration of the tournament.

It is also important to note that research clearly indicates that rolling prior to mowing will *not* result in an enhancement of green speed that is likely to be detected by the average golfer. Therefore, on golf courses that do not normally roll, it is imperative that the crew understand that the mowing *must* take place prior to the rolling to achieve the maximum green speed benefit that rolling provides.

Rolling and Double Cutting

There are two different ways to utilize a combination of rolling and double cutting. The first is obvious: double cut and follow with a lightweight rolling. Most of us would anticipate a substantial increase in green speed by combining these two proven cultural practices. Unfortunately, there is no data in the literature that allows us to predict the magnitude of the increase in green speed. Turfgrass researchers at the University of Arizona performed an intriguing study with different combinations of mowing and rolling frequencies on Tifgreen 328 Bermudagrass. The study was devised to test cultural management programs that would allow for the immediate reduction in mowing height from $5/32$ to $\frac{1}{8}$ inch. Therefore, in the experiment, the first mowing was at $5/32$ inch, followed by a rolling and then a second mowing at $\frac{1}{8}$ inch. Clearly, the study does not exactly fit our scenario, but it is interesting to note that the double-mowed–rolled plots did not result in green speeds faster than the single-mowed–rolled plots or the double-mowed–double-rolled plots. It is possible that combining the two practices may not meaningfully increase green speed, as it may have reached the point of diminishing returns. This is when taking green speed measurements on a green or two prior to and after each mowing and rolling can give the superintendent some very valuable information. Certainly, there is no reason to go through such a labor-intensive practice if it is not going to produce the desired result.

The other, less obvious, method of combining these cultural practices is to alternate daily between double cutting and lightweight rolling. Under certain conditions, this management scheme might allow the superintendent some flexibility with scheduling in preparing for a tournament. Some of the lightweight rollers discussed in Chapter 9 produced green speed increases greater than 1 foot 6 inches, with the possibility that a noticeable decrease in green speed would follow the next day (which may be influenced by thatch thickness). However, if double cutting were practiced the day following lightweight rolling, the speed increase generated by the rolling would most likely be maintained.

Silica

Data has indicated that applications of silica on seashore paspalum may lead to enhanced wear tolerance of the turf which may be attributed to increased turgor pressure of the turfgrass leaves (Trenholm et al., 2001). For this reason, it is assumed that silica might enhance green speed, but, unfortunately, no study has tested this notion. If silica does improve wear tolerance, it may be worth using prior to a tournament. Clearly, more data is needed on this subject.

Pin Placement

Fair pin placements were among the driving factors behind the creation of the Stimpmeter, but during tournaments, pins are often placed in difficult, if not impossible, positions on every green. Therefore, if you have increased your green speed for a tournament, remember that pin placements that were previously difficult may be nearly impossible with the increased speed. It is a good idea to practice putting from several locations toward the desired pin placement before cutting the cup to make sure the ball can stop 2 feet from it. Remember, not everyone wants superslick greens (which is why I am such an advocate of the "Morris Method" of finding the ideal green speed).

Incidentally, I have heard of some superintendents who mark the hole locations with a spot of paint a week before the member guest. Then they inform the members in case they want to practice putting to that location. This probably isn't fair, but we'll just call it a privilege of membership.

11

~~~~~

Filling in the Missing Pieces

*It is a question if we are not making too much of the
putting in the interests of the game, but whether we are or
not, the demand is for true uniform surfaces, and the
convener of the greens committee hears more of his
incompetence in the maintenance of putting greens than
he does of weedkilling or keeping a good fairway. Very
well—if good putting greens are wanted, how are they to
be got? Obviously applying the knowledge that exists and
by seeking for more knowledge.*
SIR ROBERT GREIG, 1929.

To Green Committee and Owners

Golf course superintendents who have sought green speed information
in an effort to accommodate their clientele have most likely been informed that

1. Speed kills
2. You must get your members to lower their expectations
3. You should deceive the golfers about your management practices
   and/or falsify your green speeds (i.e., lie) to protect your turf.

Unfortunately, none of the suggestions offer advice on *how* to balance
green speed demands with turfgrass health, and all have persisted in part
due to the lack of a comprehensive source of green speed information.

In 1929, Sir Robert Greig wrote regarding the need for proper putting
green maintenance practice research: "The first problem then is to get
together the knowledge that does exist and make it available to all"

(Anonymous, 1929). In terms of green speed issues, that is the intention of this book.

The introduction to this book begins with the statement, "Speed does not kill grass! Haste, ignorance, stubbornness, complacency, and rash un-informed decisions may kill grass, but speed does not." The chapters that followed have given a history of green speed, a method to determine a golf course's ideal green speed, data on green speed regarding various environmental and cultural impacts, and analogies intended to make the data more interesting and easier to revisit.

The data within the text will certainly challenge some people's ideas regarding green speed. And although I am certain that it contains a great deal of information, there are many missing pieces to the green speed puzzle that need to be discovered. It is precisely for this reason that I highly advocate the daily collection of green speed measurements on every golf course that has clientele concerned about this issue. If your course does not own a Stimpmeter or a Pelzmeter (Figure 11-1), purchase one. As a member of a green committee or as an owner of a golf course, you play an important role in making certain that the quest for speed does not cause undue stress on turf.

To the Superintendent

In 1929, Greig noted: "Times have changed, and a good player wants now to have a reasonable chance to hole a 10-foot putt, a feat which would have been a pure fluke in earlier days." With the changing times, Greig reasoned there was a need for "scientific research to add to the existing knowledge and fill up the blanks in our ignorance. This is an operation that will never cease" (Anonymous, 1929).

Continuing education through monthly local chapter meetings is important for the superintendent of the golf course for several reasons:

1. The superintendent gets the chance to talk to other professionals in his or her area in order to stay informed about the latest developments. During a season of excessive rain or drought, this can be extremely helpful.

2. The superintendent has an opportunity to hear a presentation on recent research findings and, just as important, to speak up and

FIGURE 11-1. *The PelzMeter is a relative newcomer as a device for measuring green speed. It comes complete with three ramps, each having an individual ball release mechanism, two levels, a calculator, three balls, a tape measure, and a carrying case. Its unique design generally results in an extremely precise grouping as the three balls come to rest.*

voice an opinion on what research remains to be done. As a turf-grass researcher myself, I can assure you that comments of this type do not fall on deaf ears.

3. By attending a meeting or golf outing, the superintendent assists in generating money to fund future research efforts.

Bill Murray, in his portrayal of Carl in Caddy Shack, exemplifies the superintendent stereotype as a worthless daydreamer with few other options in life. Although I have yet to come across a superintendent who doesn't enjoy the movie and his portrayal, no representation could be further from the truth.

Many superintendents began their careers in finance and have a business degree but later returned to college to earn a Turfgrass Management Certificate or an Associates Degree. Others knew from a young age they wanted to run a golf course and earned a bachelor's or graduate-level degree in horticulture or crop and soil sciences in pursuit of their dreams. Others have simply worked on golf courses their whole lives, enjoying the combination of art, science, and business that the job entails.

Regardless of the path the superintendent has traveled to his profession, it is my hope that by consolidating factual green speed information, this book will assist in the continuing education of golf course superintendents everywhere and will allow them to take control of green speed on their course.

Bibliography

Agnew, M. L. and J. L. Schmidt. 1992. Micronutrient study on putting greens. *1992 Iowa Turfgrass Research Report* 113–118.

Albaugh, J. 1983. A new turf menace. *USGA Green Section Record* 21(2):11–12.

Anonymous. 1928. As we find them. *Bulletin of the United States Golf Association Green Section* 8(12).

Anonymous. 1929a. *Bulletin of the United States Golf Association Green Section* 9(1):15.

Anonymous. 1929b. Research work planned in Great Britain. *Bulletin of the United States Golf Association Green Section* 9(6):106–108.

Anonymous. 1947. Mowing survey report. *Timely Turf Topics* (October):2–3.

Anonymous. 1971. Triplex putting green mowers. *USGA Green Section Record* 9(3):1–6.

Beard, J. B. 1973. *Turfgrass Science and Culture*. Englewod Cliffs, NJ: Prentice-Hall. N.J.

Beard, J. 1994. In search of the ultimate putting green. *Greenkeeper International* (December):22–25.

Beard, J. B. 1998. Fast putting surfaces cause major cultural change. TURFAX 6(2):1–2, 5.

Blais, P. 1991. Golf course superintendent's 10 deadly problems. *Holes Notes* 20(6):8–9.

Busey, P. 2001. Speeds vary little among new Bermudagrass types. *Golf Course Management* 69(2):70–73.

Christians, N. 1998. *Fundamentals of Turfgrass Management*. Chelsea, MI: Ann Arbor Press.

Christians, N. E., D. P. Martin, and J. F. Wilkinson. 1979. Nitrogen, phosphorous, and potassium effects on quality and growth of Kentucky bluegrass and creeping bentgrass. *Agronomy Journal* 71:564–567.

Colt, H. S. 1906. Treatment and upkeep of a golf course on light inland soil. London: 62–90. Country Life, Ltd. and George Newnes, Ltd., *Golf Greens and Green-keeping.*

Dennison, M. 2000. Double-cut trouble. *Golf Course Management* 68(9):80.

Dest, W. M., and K. Guillard. 2001. Bentgrass response to K fertilization and K release rates from eight sand rootzone sources used in putting green construction. *Int. Turf. Soc. Res. J.* 9:375–381.

DiPaola, J. M., and C. R. Hartwiger. 1994. Ball roll distance, rolling and soil compaction. *Golf Course Management* 62(9):49–51, 78.

Duich, J. M. 1983. Management factors affecting putting ball roll distance. *53rd Annual Michigan Turfgrass Conference* Proceedings. Vol. 12. East Lansing, MI: 76–77.

Duich, J. M., and S. Langlois. 1985. Management factors affecting green speed. *Newsnotes* (Michigan Turfgrass Foundation) (Jan/Feb/March):6–7.

Foth, H. D. 1978. Fundamentals of soil science 6th ed. New York: John Wiley & Sons, Inc.

Foth H. D., and B. G. Ellis. 1988. *Soil Fertility*. New York: John Wiley & Sons, Inc.

Garman, W. L. 1952. Permeability of various grades of sand and peat mixtures of these with soil and vermiculite. USGA J. Turf Manag. 5(1):27–28.

Gibbs, R. J., C. Liu, M.-H. Yang, and M. P. Wringley. 2000. Effect of rootzone composition and cultivation/aeration treatment on surface characteristics of golf greens under New Zealand conditions. *Journal of Turfgrass Science* (76):37–52.

Grant, J., F. Rossi, E. Gussack, and E. Nelson. 2001. Mowing height effect on disease incidence and severity in golf course turf. Cornell Turfgrass Field Day '01: Program Bookletz, 24–28.

Grau, F. V. 1933. Drift and speed of putted ball on bents as determined by mechanical putter. *Bulletin of the United States Golf Association Green Section* 13(3):74–81.

Happ, K. 2003. Putting surface pace. *USGA Green Section Record* 41(4):16–20.

Hamilton, G. W., Jr., D. W. Livingston, and A. E. Grover. 1994. The effects of lightweight rolling on putting greens. London: E. & F. N. Spon *Science and Golf II*:425–230.

Hammerschmidt, R. 1999. Phytoalexins: What have we learned after 60 years? *Annu. Rev. Phytopathol.* 37:285–306.

Harban, W. S., A. J. Hood, A. E. McCordic, A. D. Wilson, J. L. Taylor, W. C. Ferguson, W. M. Brooks, N. S. Campbell, E. F. Loeffler, W. J. Rockerfeller, F. C. Hood, S. Sherman, T. P. Hinman, and C. B. Buxton. 1922. How frequently should putting greens be mowed? A discussion. Bulletin of the Green Section of the U.S. Golf Association. 2(3):92-96.

Hartwiger, C. 1996. The ups and down of rolling putting greens. *UDGA Green Section Record* 34(4):1-4.

Hartwiger, C. E., C. H. Peacock, J. M. DiPaola, M. Joseph, and K. D. Cassel. 2001. Impact of light-weight rolling on putting green performance. *Crop Science* 41(4):1179-1184.

Hoos, D. D., and W. W. Faust. 1979. Putting greens—the height of cut. *USGA Green Section Record* 17(4):1-4.

Hummel, N. W. 1993. Rationale for revisions of the USGA green construction specifications. *USGA Green Section Record* (March/April):7-21.

Hutchinson, H. G. 1906. *Golf Greens and Green-keeping.* London: Country Life, Ltd. and George Newnes, Ltd.

Isaac, S. P., and P. M. Canaway. 1987. The mineral nutrition of Festuca-Agrostis golf greens: A review. *J. Sports Turf Res. Inst.* 63:9-27.

Karcher, D., T. Nikolai, and R. Calhoun. 2001. Golfer's perception of green speeds vary. *Golf Course Management* 69(3):57-60.

Karcher, D. E., T. A. Nikolai, and P. E. Rieke. 1996. The HydroJect: Not just an aerifier. *Proceedings of the 66th Annual Michigan Turfgrass Conference* 25:119-121.

Kerr, D. E., D. M. Kopec, T. E. Ruhl, and J. J. Golbert. 2001. Cultural management for height reduction of Tifgreen 328 Bermudagrass greens. *Turfgrass, Landscape, and Urban IPM Research Summary.* 8th ed., 173-178.

Knoop, William. 2000. Low mowing height lowdown. *Southern Golf* 31(2):10, 23.

Kussow, W. R. 1998. Putting green management systems. *Wisconsin Turf Research: Results of 1998 Studies* (16):85-93.

Labbance, B., and G. Witteveen. 2002. Keepers of the green: A history of golf course management. Chelsea, MI: Ann Arbor Press.

Langlois, S. R. 1985. Practices affecting putting green speed. Master's thesis, Department of Agronomy, Pennsylvania State University.

Lees, P. W. 1918. *Care of the Green.* New York: C. B. Wilcox.

Lodge, T. A. 1992. A study of the effects of golf green construction and differential irrigation and fertiliser nutrition rates on golf ball behavior. *J. Sports Turf Res. Inst.* 68:95-103.

Lodge, T. A., and S. W. Baker. 1991. The construction, irrigation, and fertiliser nutrition of golf greens. II. Playing quality the first year of differential irrigation and nutrition treatments. *J. Sports Turf Res. Inst.* 67(June): 44-52.

Mackie, John. 1929. A professional's view of turf problems. *Bulletin of the United States Golf Association Green Section* 9(2):32-34.

Marschner, H. 1995. *Mineral Nutrition of Higher Plants*. 2nd ed. San Diego, CA: Academic Press.

Metcalf, M. M. 1922. Treatment for unwatered greens. *Bulletin of the Green Section of the United States Golf Association*. 2(7):209-210.

Mitchell, R. V. 1983. It's a good tool—Use with caution and restraint. *USGA Green Section Record* 21(2):13-16.

Monteith, J., Jr. 1928. The Arlington Turf Garden. *The Bulletin of the United States Golf Association Green Section* 8(12):244-245.

Monteith, J., Jr. 1929. Testing turf with a mechanical putter. *The Bulletin of the United States Golf Association Green Section* 9(1):3-6.

Morris, Jike. Verbal communication, January 23, 2002 Michigan Turfgrass Foundation Conference.

Nus, J., and P. Haupt. 1989. Effect of mowing height and potassium fertilization on quality parameters of Pencross creeping bentgrass. *1989 Turfgrass Research* (Kansas State University) (June):29-32.

Oakley, R. A. 1925. Fertilizers in relation to quality of turf and to weed control. *Bulletin* of the Green Section of the United States Golf Association. 5(3):50-56.

Oakley, R. A. 1926. Why fescue does not make good putting turf. *Bulletin of the United States Golf Association Green Section* 6(2):47.

Ostmeyer, T. 2003. New age: The fundamental maintenance practice of aerification isn't what it used to be. *Golf Course Management* 71(3):74-76, 78-80, 82-84, 86.

Piper, C. V., and R. A. Oakley. 1921. Rolling the turf. Bulletin of the Green Section of the U.S. Golf Association. 1(3):36.

Potter, D. A. 1998. *Destructive Turfgrass Insects: Biology, Diagnosis, and Control*. Chelsea, MI: Ann Arbor Press.

Puhalla, J., J. Krans, and M. Goatley. 1999. *Sports Turf: A Manual for Design, Construction and Maintenance*. Chelsea, MI: Ann Arbor Press.

Radko, A. M. 1973. Refining green section specifications for putting green construction. Proceedings of the Second International Turfgrass Research Conference. American Society of Agronomy and Crop Science Society of America with the International Turfgrass Society. Madison, WI.

Radko, A. M. 1977. How fast are your greens? *USGA Green Section Record* 15(5):10-11.

Radko, A. M. 1978. How fast are your greens? An update. *USGA Green Section Record* 16(2):20-21.

Radko, A. M. 1985. Have we gone too far with low nitrogen on greens? *USGA Green Section Record* 23(2):26-28.

Radko, A. M., Engel, R. E., and Trout, R. E. 1981. A study of putting green variability. *USGA Green Section Record* 19(1):9-13.

Rieke, P. E., M. T. McElroy, and L. Douglas. 1988. 1987 turfgrass soil research report. *Proceedings of the 58th Annual Michigan Turfgrass Conference* (17):4-8.

Rist, A. M., and Roch E. Gaussoin. 1997. Mowing isn't sole factor in affecting ball-roll distance. *Golf Course Management* 65(6):49-54.

Rogers, J. N., III, T. A. Nikolai, and J. A. Rea. 1992. The effect of plant growth regulators on putting green speed and quality. *Proceedings of the 62nd Annual Michigan Turfgrass Conference* 21:3-6.

Salaiz, T. A., G. L. Horst, and R. C. Sherman. 1995. Mowing height and vertical mowing frequency effects on putting green quality. *Crop Science* 35(5): 1422-1425.

Sartain, J. B. 2002. Tifway Bermudagrass response to potassium fertilization. *Crop Science* 42:507-512.

Scott, J. L. 1998. The big show: Hosting a professional tournament can be a challenging and rewarding experience for a superintendent. *Golf Course Management* 66(7):122-124.

Smiley, R. W. 1983. *Compendium of Turfgrass Diseases*. St. Paul, MN: American Phytopathological Society.

Sprague, H. B., and E. E. Evaul. 1930. *Experiments with Turf Grasses in New Jersey*. New Jersey Agricultural Experiment Station Bulletin No. 497. New Brunswick: New Jersey Agricultural Experiment Station.

Stahnke, G. K., and J. B. Beard. 1981. The effect of cultural practices on the surface speed of closely mowed greens. *Texas Turfgrass Research—1979-80*. (January):60-63.

Stimpson, E. 1937. Introducing the Stimp. *Golfdom: The Business Journal of Golf* 11(2):40-41, 44.

Stimpson, E. S. 1974. Putting greens—How fast? *Golf Journal* 27(2):28-29.

Streich, A., and R. Gaussoin. 2000. Topdressing and ball roll. *Grounds Maintenance* 35(1):40, 44, 48.

Thomas, Frank W. 1983. How it all began. *USGA Green Section Record* 21(2):10-11.

Throssell, Clark. 1981. Management factors affecting putting green speed. Master's thesis, Pennsylvania State University.

Throssell, Clark. 1985. Management practices affecting bentgrass putting green speed. *CPTF Newsletter* (March/April):2-3.

Tiziani, Mario. 1990. Natural variation in putting green speed. *Grass Roots* 17(1):11–14.

Travis, W. J. 1901. *Practical Golf.* New York: Harper & Brothers.

Trenholm, L. E., R. R. Duncan, R. N. Carrow, and G. H. Snyder. 2001. Influence of silica on growth, quality, and wear tolerance of seashore paspalum. *Journal of Plant Nutrition* 24(2):245–259.

Turgeon, A. J. 1991. *Turfgrass Management.* 3rd ed. Englewood Cliffs, NJ: Prentice-Hall.

USA Today. "USA Today Snapshots," by April Umminger and Dave Merrill, May 16, 2002.

USGA Green Section Staff. 1960. Specifications for a method of putting green construction. Far Hills, NJ: U.S. Golf Association.

USGA Green Section Staff. 1965. Turf Twisters. *USGA Green Section Record* 2(5).

USGA Green Section Staff. 1996. *Stimpmeter Instruction Booklet.* Far Hills, NJ: USGA Golf House.

USGA Green Section Staff. 2003. Turf Twisters. *USGA Green Section Record* 41(6).

Vargas, J. M., Jr. 1994. Management of Turfgrass Diseases. 2nd ed. Boca Raton, FL: Lewis Publishers.

White, Charles B. 1985. How low can you mow bermudagrass greens? *Proceedings of the 33rd Annual Florida Turf-Grass Conference* 33:39–41.

Williams, D. W., and A. J. Powell Jr. 1995. Dew removal and dollar spot on creeping bentgrass. *Golf Course Management* 63(8):49–52.

Yelverton, F. H. 1998. Effects of trinexapac-ethyl and paclobutrazol on ball roll and summer stress of creeping bentgrass. *Southern Weed Science Society Proceedings* 51:68.

About the Author

Dr. Thomas A. Nikolai is the Turfgrass Academic Specialist at Michigan State University. His duties include teaching various courses: Introduction to Turf, Golf Course Irrigation, Turf and Landscape Analytical Practices, Turf and the Environment, and Basic Soils. Dr. Nikolai is also a faculty member of the Golf Course Superintendents Association of America (GCSAA) specializing in the issues of green speed management.

Before becoming an instructor, Dr. Nikolai spent ten years working on golf courses (three as a superintendent and two as an assistant) and ten years working as a turfgrass research technician. He draws on his past experiences in the classroom and has been voted the "2003 Outstanding Faculty Member" by his students. While he was a research technician, his topics of study included fertilization, topdressing, lightweight green rolling, cultivation techniques, plant growth regulators (PGRs), mowing heights, wetting agents, leaf mulching, irrigation scheduling, putting green root zone mixes, and alternative spikes. For many of these studies Dr. Nikolai collected green speed data with the Stimpmeter and is renowned for his knowledge regarding green speed issues.

Index

145